MW01069800

SHADOW RIDGE MIDDLE SCHOOL
MEDIA CENTER
12551 HOLLY STREET
THORNTON, COLORADO 80241
LEXILE LEVEL

# *Gidgets* and WOMEN WARRIORS

## PERCEPTIONS OF WOMEN IN THE 1950S AND 1960S

### *Catherine Gourley*

Twenty-First Century Books • Minneapolis

*For Marguerite,*
*a "sister" who grew up next door*
*and remembers it all*

Text copyright © 2008 by Catherine Gourley

Twenty-First Century Books
A division of Lerner Publishing Group, Inc.
241 First Avenue North
Minneapolis, MN  55401 U.S.A.

Website address: www.lernerbooks.com


Library of Congress Cataloging-in-Publication Data

Gourley, Catherine, 1950–
    Gidgets and women warriors : perceptions of women in the 1950s and 1960s / by Catherine Gourley.
        p.   cm. — (Images and issues of women in the twentieth century)
    Includes bibliographical references and index.
    ISBN-13: 978–0–8225–6805–6 (lib. bdg. : alk. paper)
    1. Women—United States—History—20th century. 2. Women—United States—Social conditions—20th century. 3. Women—United States—Social life and customs—20th century. 4. Women in popular culture—United States—History—20th century. 5. Popular culture—United States—History—20th century. 6. Nineteen fifties. 7. Nineteen sixties. I. Title.
HQ1420.G674  2008
305.40973'09045—dc22                                                                2006036103

Manufactured in the United States of America
1 2 3 4 5 6 – JR– 13 12 11 10 09 08

# Contents

*Who did this young woman of the 1950s see when she looked into the mirror? Was she Gidget of TV and movie fame, looking forward to a good time at the beach? Or would she follow the era's new opportunities for women?*

SHADOW RIDGE MEDIA CENTER

# AUTHOR'S NOTE

A favorite television program of my childhood was *I Love Lucy*. Lucy Ricardo and Ethel Mertz were screwball housewives who invented outrageous schemes for earning money, meeting celebrities, and getting into show business. Although Lucy's conspiracies usually failed, each episode ended with her husband Ricky proclaiming his love for his wacky wife.

When I was growing up in the 1950s and 1960s, most television images of moms portrayed them wearing frilly aprons and pearls while dusting the furniture. My mom, however, worked outside the home. I never saw her in a frilly apron, and dusting the furniture was *my* chore. Although she laughed at Lucy's antics, my mom was no Lucy Ricardo. Mom managed her own money and never turned on the tears to wheedle my father into giving her what she wanted.

Not until years later did I learn the truth about the real Lucy. Lucille Ball, the actress and Hollywood producer, wasn't goofy. She had brains as well as beauty. She was the first woman to head a major television production studio. Looking back, I realize my mom was more like that real Lucy. She was not a Hollywood star, and she didn't own her

*"Sales Resistance" is the name of an* I Love Lucy *episode in which Ricky insists that Lucy (above) get rid of a vacuum cleaner she bought from a door-to-door salesman. Lucy may look defeated—but her viewers eventually learned to trust that she always comes out on top.*

own business. Still, she had Lucy's independence and determination.

This book is the fourth in a series on women's images and issues in the twentieth century. It focuses on the decades of the 1950s and 1960s. To research the book, I traveled back in time. Specifically, I hunted for answers to two questions: How did the popular media of the past portray women? Were those images of women accurate or misleading?

An image can be visual, such as a photograph, a painting, or a film. But images can also be print documents, including letters, newspaper articles, short stories, and novels. In searching for women's images and the issues important to women during the 1950s and 1960s, I read women's and teen magazines. I hunted for news stories about women who made headlines by flying jets at supersonic speeds or taking stands against segregation and racism in their schools and communities. I watched reruns of early television situation comedies and dozens of TV commercials. I listened to the rock-and-roll music of the 1950s and the girl groups of the early 1960s. My research was part of the journey, and I loved it.

Throughout the twentieth century, media images—whether fact or fiction, stereotypical or sensationalized—influenced women's perception of themselves. But women did not always accept these images blindly. The conflicting images of popular culture and the ways women reacted to those images is what this series is all about. As you read, you too will travel back in time. I hope you'll return to the present with greater understanding of how popular culture may have influenced your mother, your grandmother, perhaps even your great-grandmother. More important, I hope you'll see yourself reflected within these pages and understand that you—not society—hold the paintbrush that creates the person you become.

—*Catherine Gourley*

# the lady from maine addresses the senate: june 1, 1950

*Senator Margaret Chase Smith in San Francisco, California, July 13, 1964*

*I was young. I was a woman.*
*I worried that it was presumptuous of me*
*to tell everyone else they were wrong.*

—Senator Margaret Chase Smith, 1964

# Margaret Chase Smith was nervous.

She was about to make the most important speech of her life, on the floor of the U.S. Senate. Although she was a senator from Maine, she had never before spoken in front of her peers. Most of the senators seated at their desks were more experienced than she was. And they were all male. But that wasn't why butterflies batted inside her stomach and her hands trembled. The cause of her anxiety was the speech itself, the words she had written and rewritten over the previous few days. What she was about to tell her fellow senators could mean the end of her own political career.

She looked over her shoulder. Her aide Bill Lewis stood at the back of the Senate chamber, waiting. He held two hundred copies of the senator's speech. Once Senator Smith began speaking, he would begin to distribute the copies to members of the press in the second-floor gallery. Smith might also have glanced nervously at Senator Joseph McCarthy, seated just two rows behind her. Many senators and representatives in the nation's capital feared him. Smith, too, thought he was a dangerous man.

Earlier that morning, Senator McCarthy had approached her at the Senate subway station. "You look serious, Margaret," he said. "Are you about to make a speech?"

"Yes," she admitted, "and you will not like it."

"Is it about me?"

"Yes."

"Remember," he warned, "I am a powerful man." Senator McCarthy had recently accused a number of people in government positions of being Communists. Communists support the Communist political system, the type of government used by a U.S. enemy of the era, the Soviet Union (then fifteen republics, including Russia). Senator McCarthy's accusations had made headline news and threatened to ruin the careers of the people he had accused.

Seated at her desk in the Senate chamber, Margaret Chase Smith considered changing her mind. The president of the Senate (the nation's vice president) had not yet called on her to speak. Her aide had not yet distributed the copies of her speech. There was still time. But her conscience would not allow her to back down. She must speak, no matter the consequences.

A short time later, her opportunity came. Senator Smith's hands still trembled as she stood. "Mr. President, I would like to speak briefly and simply about a serious national condition," she began. Her voice was so quiet that many of the senators leaned forward to hear her. "It is a national feeling of fear and frustration that could result in national suicide and the end of everything that we Americans hold dear."

According to plan, Bill Lewis began passing out the copies of Senator Smith's speech. There was no turning back.

She was shocked by events of the last few months, the senator said. Bullies in the Senate were attempting to seize greater political power. How? By spreading seeds of fear and suspicion about innocent people. The bullies accused anyone who criticized the U.S. government of being a Communist. She explained that Communists oppose capitalism and democracy, and many of them at that time wanted to overthrow the U.S. government. She agreed that Communism was a threat to the American way of life, but the bullies were making their accusations without any concrete evidence. She said that these malicious rumors had ruined the lives of the accused and their families.

Senator Smith did not mention any names, but everyone in the Senate chamber knew of whom she was speaking. The bullies were Senator McCarthy and those who supported him. Upstairs in the press gallery, reporters turned to one another, somewhat bewildered. Not even reporter May Craig had known the senator was going to give a speech. Craig wrote for the news media in Maine. She and Senator Smith were friends. But Craig was also friendly with Senator McCarthy and strongly supported his hunt for Communists. And so Margaret Chase Smith had kept her speech a secret, even from May Craig. By then other reporters were leaning forward, some over the balcony railing, to hear more clearly what the soft-spoken senator below was saying.

"The American people are sick and tired of being afraid to speak

*May Craig (right) was a strong supporter of equal opportunities for women and had blazed many trails as a female journalist during World War II (1939–1945). Craig was a friend of Senator Margaret Chase Smith and wrote for newspapers in Smith's home state of Maine. Craig is shown here with Senator McCarthy outside his office in 1954.*

their minds," she stated. "Freedom of speech is not what it used to be in America." The false accusations were wrong, she said. But worse was that government leaders, both Democrats and Republicans, had done nothing at all to stop the bullies' scare-and-smear tactics. She was not proud of her fellow senators' behavior, she said. Instead, she felt shame. And so she had written a declaration of conscience. Six senators had privately read the declaration and had also signed it. "It is high time that we stopped thinking politically as Republicans and Democrats . . ." she challenged, "and started thinking patriotically as Americans."

Her speech lasted fifteen minutes. And then she sat down. An uneasy murmuring swirled about the chamber. The senators and the press turned their attention to the unnamed bully Senator Smith had just attacked. Joseph McCarthy was glaring at her. Instead of firing back, however, as he had done so many times before in public meetings, he surprised everyone. He walked out of the Senate without saying a word.

The "lady from Maine," as the press called Smith, had won the day.

*Margaret Chase Smith's speech* on June 1, 1950, was controversial. She had attacked a powerful and outspoken senator when no one else seemingly had the courage to do so. And she had dared to criticize the U.S. government and those leaders who were not protecting the basic rights of citizens. The next morning, the *New York Times*

*Senator Margaret Chase Smith delivered what was to be known as her declaration of conscience speech to the U.S. Senate on June 1, 1950. In it, she criticized Senator Joseph McCarthy for his vicious political attacks against alleged U.S. Communists. After the speech, McCarthy and his staff nicknamed her Moscow Maggie, in reference to the Soviet capital.*

COMM... RTY ORGANIZATION U.S.A-FEB. 9, 1950

*Wisconsin senator Joseph McCarthy is shown here in front of a map charting alleged Communist activity in the United States. In mid-1954, Americans watched televised hearings in which McCarthy made wild and sometimes unfounded accusations of Communist conspiracy against American citizens. By the end of the year, the Senate censured (officially reprimanded) McCarthy for abuse of legislative powers. Even so, many lives and careers had been ruined by McCarthy's relentless pursuit of those he deemed Communists.*

printed her photograph on page one with a headline that read, "Senators Decry 'Smear' Tactics of McCarthy." "Attack led by Mrs. Smith of Maine . . . ," the newspaper reported. Across the country, other newspapers also reported the story. The *Chicago Sun-Times* called Smith the "woman of the hour." In Florida the *St. Augustine Record* called her a true "statesman." The publisher of the *Washington Post* described her speech as "magnificent." One reporter sent her a bouquet of roses, and thousands of Americans sent her letters, applauding the stand she had taken.

Not all reactions were favorable, however.

Some Americans accused Smith of being unpatriotic. A few suggested that she herself might be a Communist. Publicly, an indignant Joseph McCarthy mocked Smith and the other senators who had signed her declaration of conscience. He called them "Snow White and the six dwarfs." He made it clear that he would continue his investigation into the lives of any and every U.S. citizen he suspected of being a Communist.

Smith's speech was controversial for still another reason. She was a woman.

In the United States in the 1950s, most women were housewives and mothers. They were not doctors, lawyers, or scientists. And they certainly were not politicians. Margaret Chase Smith had been the first woman ever elected to the U.S. Senate. One government leader admitted that if a man had given the same speech, he would have become the nation's next president. *Newsweek* didn't go quite that far, but it published a photograph of Smith on its cover with the caption, "Senator Smith: A Woman Vice President?"

In the 1950s, the threat of a nuclear attack from the Soviet Union was very real for every schoolchild. Classrooms routinely had duck-and-cover drills in which the children were instructed to move away from windows and crouch down, preferably under a desk.

To understand the controversy surrounding Smith and her declaration of conscience speech requires a small step back in time. A decade earlier, the United States and its allies fought World War II (1939–1945). The enemy was the armies of Adolf Hitler of Germany, Benito Mussolini of Italy, and the emperor of Japan. To end the war, the United States dropped two atomic bombs on Japan, one on the city of Hiroshima and the other on Nagasaki. In an instant, those two terrifying explosions had obliterated the cities and killed hundreds of thousands of people. The new, top-secret atomic weapon had brought an end to World War II. It also changed the world forever.

After the war, the United States began fighting the Cold War (1945–1991). In the 1950s, no army had invaded U.S. shores. Yet the fear of another world war was like a dark cloud on the horizon. The enemy was the Soviet Union. It had begun testing its own atomic weapons. Americans feared the Soviet Communists would use the atomic bomb to start a third world war.

The best defense against Communism and war, argued some U.S. leaders, was not a weapon at all. The best defense was the American family. And women had a vital role to play. During World War II, the U.S. government had encouraged women to do their patriotic duty—to leave their homes and work in war industries to build airplanes and ships. Patriotism included buying war bonds and planting vegetables in backyard victory gardens. Patriotism also meant rationing food and recycling tin cans and rubber tires. But the war ended and the Cold War began, and that changed the United States' definition of patriotism. The country's expectations for women also changed.

The government encouraged women to give up their career ambitions. A woman's place was in the home, not in a government office or a science laboratory. Jobs belonged to the male soldiers returning from war. Patriotism was finding a husband. Popular media in the 1950s provided countless tips on how a young woman could do just that—everything from bathing with a certain brand of soap to styling her hair correctly. Society generally viewed women who didn't marry as unhappy spinsters. Again, popular media promoted this idea. "Raise Your Girl to Be a Wife" was the title of an article in *Parents* magazine in 1956. Women might go to

*Rosie the Riveter* (above) *was introduced by the Office of War Information in 1942. During World War II, women were encouranged to care for home and children, plant victory gardens, and buy war bonds. The were also encouraged to hold down a full-time job, preferably in the defense industry.*

college, but society emphasized that the purpose of a woman's education was not to advance her own career but rather to help her husband advance his. And her education could help her raise healthy and happy children. At all-female Smith College in Massachusetts, presidential candidate Adlai Stevenson told the graduates of 1955, "This assignment for you, as wives and mothers, you can do in the living room with a baby in your lap or in the kitchen with a can opener in your hand."

"There is no question that the social pressure to appear mature, responsible . . . [and] patriotic contributed to the rush into marriage," wrote historian Elaine Tyler May. Women began marrying at a younger age, many right after high school graduation. The glamorous movie star Elizabeth Taylor was eighteen when she married for the first time, in 1950. Photographs of the smiling bride appeared in magazines across the country. Even cartoon characters were getting "hitched." In earlier decades, Li'l Abner, Dick Tracy, and the boxing champion Joe Palooka were bachelors. In the 1950s, they not only became husbands, but they became daddies.

*Marriage was big in the early 1950s. Al Capp's title character Li'l Abner had been successfully avoiding marriage since the comic strip first appeared in 1934. But in March 1952, Li'l Abner went to the altar (above).*

In the 1950s, patriotism meant having babies—and more than one! The U.S. birthrate soared in the prosperous postwar years.

Patriotism also meant living in new, ranch-style houses in suburban neighborhoods and purchasing U.S.-made gadgets, including automobiles, televisions, refrigerators, and washing machines. Purchasing products was patriotic, the popular media suggested, because spending kept factories and industries profitable and provided jobs for Americans. Advertisers also claimed that modern conveniences would make the American housewife's life easier and give her plenty of "togetherness" time with her growing family. In this way, American women could raise a new generation of confident children who believed in and would defend democracy. Housewives and mothers were the "architects of peace," wrote author Louise Crandall Church in *American Home*. Of course, not every American family could afford to buy the gleaming gadgets of the postwar era. Nevertheless, marriage, motherhood, and owning a house were American ideals of the time.

The Cold War and patriotism weren't the only social issues that influenced women's lives in the 1950s and 1960s. Teenagers emerged as a cultural phenomenon. Teenage girls, in particular, had money to spend. They made cultural icons of rock-and-roll performers. They influenced fashion, advertising, and popular culture. In doing so, they challenged society's understanding of what femininity was. *Gidget* was the title of a novel published in the 1950s about a

*Motherhood was a woman's destiny in the 1950s, and the women's magazines did all they could to idealize the image. This cover photo of a beautiful baby and his perfectly made-up mother in a lace robe resting on a white silk pillow was not practical. But it sold magazines.*

San Francisco, California

*At the same time that* Good Housekeeping *was still going strong among mainstream women, the Daughters of Bilitis, the nation's first lesbian rights organization, started publishing* The Ladder. The Ladder *helped lesbians claim an identity and form a feminist consciousness before the women's liberation movement.*

For many young women, Gidget was a symbol of liberation and daring.

Before she ran for the Senate, Margaret Chase Smith had been a housewife and a mother. She had found great satisfaction in those roles. Yet she understood that women could fulfill other roles as well. When she addressed the Senate on June 1, 1950, she said, "I speak as a woman. I speak as a United States Senator. I speak as an American." In some ways, Smith was a woman warrior. She didn't fight in an army with guns and bombs. But she did fight—for social justice. Her weapons were words, wit, and wisdom.

Throughout the 1950s and 1960s, other women listened to their consciences. Like Smith, they took a stand to fight for what they believed was right. *Gidgets and Women Warriors* is part of a series of books on the images and issues that influenced American women during the twentieth century. It focuses on the decades of the 1950s and 1960s. It is a journey back in time to examine how popular culture influenced the lives of women. It is the story, too, of some of the women, such as Senator Margaret Chase Smith, who broke stereotypes and changed the way the world saw them.

teenage girl who dared to enter the men's world of surfing. The popularity of that book triggered a series of "beach blanket" films and later a television show that helped expand an already growing youth culture.

# chapter one
# the three A's of femininity

(From left) *Marilyn Monroe, Betty Grable, and Lauren Bacall in* How to Marry a Millionaire *(1953)*

*My whole philosophy of Barbie was that through the doll,*
*the little girl could be anything she wanted to be.*
*Barbie always represented the fact that a woman has choices.*

—Ruth Handler, creator of the Barbie doll, from *Dream Doll: The Ruth Handler Story*

# *a girl stands in her bedroom gazing*

into a full-length mirror. She is perhaps fourteen. She wears a plaid shirt with the sleeves rolled up past her elbows. She also wears dungarees. In a few more years, girls will call these baggy denim pants blue jeans. But not yet. This is 1949. The girl holds up a party dress, a long gown with layers of white fabric and puffy sleeves. Her closet door is open. Inside, hanging on a hook, are a pair of ice skates. On a stool is a large box with wrapping paper. The dress apparently is a new purchase.

This painting by Norman Rockwell is titled *The Prom Dress*. It appeared on the cover of a popular magazine called the *Saturday Evening Post*. The painting really shows two girls—the tomboy who wears dungarees and ice skates and the girl reflected in the mirror, pressing the frilly fabric against her shoulders. Someone liked the dress well enough to buy it for her, but the girl is not yet wearing it. In fact, she tilts her head a little to one side, as if trying to decide: Is this who I am? Is this who I want to be?

In 1954 another Norman Rockwell painting of a girl looking into a mirror appeared on the cover of the *Saturday Evening Post*. This girl is wearing a petticoat, or slip. She is barefoot and bare armed. She sits on a stool, low to the floor, her knees drawn up. She holds both hands to her chin. On the girl's lap is a photograph of a movie star. In the mirror, the girl imitates the pouting expression of the Hollywood celebrity. A doll is cast aside on the floor, as if thrown away. On the floor, too, are a comb, a brush, and an open tube of lipstick.

This painting's title is *Girl in the Mirror*. The girl seated on the stool and the one reflected in the mirror are very much the same. This girl has already decided who she wants to be. She has replaced the toys of her childhood with new objects of femininity.

Not every adolescent girl studies her image in a mirror. But it is a pretty safe bet that most girls throughout the twentieth century asked themselves the same questions: Who am I? Who do I want to become? Sometimes the answer came from within the girl herself, especially if she had a special talent for or interest in sports, music, reading, or calculating numbers and solving problems. Frequently, the answer came from a parent or a teacher who told the girl who she should become. Popular media, too, suggested how a girl might dress and behave.

The mirror that society held up to girls in the 1950s and 1960s suggested females were to be, above all else, feminine. But weren't all females already feminine? Not according to *Parents* magazine. An article from the 1950s warned mothers that "wives aren't born—they are made. Your daughter is born a female, but she has to learn how to be feminine."

*Images of femininity offered to the young girls of the 1950s were often conflicting. The sexy, frilly prom dress quickly switched to a practical, frilly apron once the goal of marriage was achieved.*

Without femininity, a girl could not attract a boy. She might never marry nor have children. Without femininity, she might discover her husband was having an affair with another woman, who was so feminine that she made him feel like a king. Femininity was a girl's key to popularity and happiness. At least, that was the message in hundreds of books, magazine articles, and movies of the times.

But just what was femininity? It can best be summed up as the three A's. In the 1950s, the first A was appearance, or how a girl looked. It was a prom dress with puffy sleeves or a well-ironed house-dress with a frilly apron.

The second A of femininity was actions, or how a girl behaved. *Seventeen* magazine asked its readers in 1960 the following questions: "Do you dominate the conversation? Do you wear your hair to please yourself rather than your boyfriend? If a boy is rude, do you scold or correct his behavior? If you do, warned *Seventeen*, you didn't rate very high on the femininity scale."

The final A of femininity was ambition—the strong desire to achieve a goal. In the 1950s, a good deal of society believed that a girl's greatest ambition was—or should be—to become a wife and mother. As a child, a boy might dream of becoming an engineer, of building bridges or skyscrapers. A girl might have the same dream, but she'd most likely do her engineering in the home, building a family. Child care experts urged mothers to teach their daughters homemaking skills, and the sooner the better! In this way, they were helping their daughters achieve their feminine ambition.

## Jackie's Decision

In the summer of 1950, Jacqueline Bouvier was touring Paris, France, with friends. She was not yet twenty-one years old. She had come to France a year earlier as a college junior to study in Paris at the Sorbonne, one of the oldest and most respected universities in Europe. Art was Jackie's passion. She spent many hours inside the Louvre and other French museums studying works of master artists. Soon she would return to the United States to complete her senior year of college.

On the surface, Jackie's life seemed ideal. She lived with her mother and wealthy stepfather on an estate called Hammersmith Farm, along the seacoast in Rhode Island. She had her own horse. She attended private schools with the children of other upperclass families. Beneath the surface, however, Jackie was unhappy. Her mother criticized her repeatedly. Jackie's eyes were set too far

By July 1949, nineteen-year-old Jacqueline Bouvier was already rethinking the idea of marriage—the third A of femininity. In two months, she would sail to France for a year of study and adventure.

apart for her face, her mother told her. Her hands and her feet were too big. She wasn't graceful and ladylike. Jackie excelled in school. But even this, her mother ridiculed. No one wants to marry a woman who is smarter than the people around her, Jackie's mother told her.

Her mother encouraged Jackie to flirt with young men by speaking in a soft, little girl voice and staring at them wide-eyed as they talked. One young man who had taken Jackie to a football game at Yale University in Connecticut said Jackie often pretended to be less intelligent than she really was. He recalled, "It'd be fourth down and five to go, she'd say to me, 'Oh, why are they kicking the ball?'... The truth is she probably knew more about football than I did."

In Paris, however, Jackie was free from her mother's critical eyes and sharp tongue. She could go where she wanted to go, do what she wanted to do, and wear whatever clothes she liked. That year in France, Jackie Bouvier discovered a truth about herself. "I learned not to be ashamed of a real hunger for knowledge, something I had always tried to hide," she said. Her year away from home had given her confidence. "I loved it more than any year of my life," she said.

Bouvier returned to the United States a stronger, more mature young woman. In her senior year in college, she won a writing contest sponsored by *Vogue* magazine. The prize was a one-year job working for the magazine, the first six months in New York City and then six months in Paris. Her mother, however, objected. "You're making the biggest mistake of your life," she told her. "You're going to be twenty-two years old in July and you're not engaged yet."

In high school, Jackie had written that she did not want to become a housewife. While she might marry one day, she also wanted a career, perhaps as an artist or a writer like those whose works she later studied in Paris. Her mother pressured her, however. Many of the young women Bouvier knew in college were engaged before graduation. After college, it was time she, too, found a husband and

*Jacqueline Bouvier poses with a Speed Graphic press camera* (left) *during her work as an inquiring photographer for the* Washington Times-Herald *in 1953. But her mother was right — Washington, D.C., was full of eligible bachelors. On September 12 of that same year, the aspiring reporter married John F. Kennedy.*

started a family. Eventually, Bouvier gave in. She wrote to the editors of *Vogue* to explain why she could not accept the prize. Her mother, she wrote, felt strongly about keeping her daughter close to home.

Bouvier did not give in completely to her mother, however. She decided not to return to Hammersmith Farm. Instead, she took a job in the nation's capital with the *Washington Times-Herald*. Someone had told her that Washington, D.C., was where all the best of the eligible young bachelors were. Had she accepted the prize and returned to Paris rather than to the nation's capital, Bouvier likely would not have met a handsome and charming young senator named John Fitzgerald Kennedy. Years later,

as his wife and as the nation's First Lady, this once-awkward little girl with a hunger for knowledge would become one of the most admired women in the United States.

## The M.R.S. Degree

During the 1950s, U.S. educators debated the same question that Jacqueline Bouvier struggled with: what should women be educated for — a career or homemaking? No one could quite agree. When tennis champion Maureen Connolly married in 1955, she gave up her sport. Connolly had dominated women's sports since she was fourteen, winning the women's title at Wimbledon in England three years in a row. She was an incredibly powerful player.

# A Spouse Trap for Susie

Thousands of young women applied each year for admission to all-female Stephens College in Columbia, Missouri. The college's course of study included music, nutrition, tap dancing, and expressive speech. During their two years at Stephens, students also learned to ride horses and play golf, activities that would serve them well once they graduated and married. The fifteen hundred students each year also took courses on dieting and how to make up their faces. They exercised daily and also took afternoon naps to maintain their youthful energy and appearances. They studied the Bible. Perhaps the

most enjoyable school activities of all were the frequent field trips they took to meet and socialize with young, single men. Adult chaperones accompanied them, of course. Very often the president of the college, James Woods, was a chaperone.

Stephens College taught women how to become feminine. Getting accepted wasn't easy. According to *Time* magazine, the school selected its students on their appearance and their "home-town popularity" rather than their high school grades. The college did not

*Stephens College girls have an off-campus class to study the shoreline of Missouri's Lake of the Ozarks.*

want to "waste its makeup, clothing and budget clinics," reported *Time*, ". . . on the hopelessly homely or the misfits."

Many educators from other institutions of higher learning criticized Woods's choice of a "feminine" curriculum. These critics referred to Stephens as a spouse trap and its graduates as Susies. Nevertheless, Stephens College remained committed to the belief that all women (the attractive ones, at least) should be educated in becoming pleasant housewives and loving mothers.

Sportswriters nicknamed her Mighty Little Mo, a reference to the powerful World War II battleship *Missouri*, known as Big Mo. And yet when the Catholic bishop married Connelly, he stated she had made the right decision in becoming queen of a home rather than queen of the courts. Connolly would tell reporters a few years later that her life as a housewife kept her so busy she didn't miss tennis. Although Connolly was a happy housewife, not all women who gave up their career ambitions were so content.

*Maureen "Little Mo" Connolly is shown here playing winning tennis at Wimbledon in 1952. The following year, she not only won Wimbledon again but also took the French, Australian, and U.S. championships, making her the first woman and the second person to win the Grand Slam.*

Smith College's president, Benjamin Fletcher Wright, believed that most educated women were frustrated, even ashamed, to be just a housewife. The fault wasn't theirs, he said. The colleges were to blame. They educated women as if they were no different from men. But they were different, Wright insisted. After graduation, men had careers in office buildings in cities. They became lawyers and ran for political office. Women graduates, on the other hand, were more likely to become household launderers, cooks, and nurses to their husbands and children.

To address the unhappiness he was certain these educated housewives experienced, Wright created a new major for Smith College females: family studies. He also began a course on family law, which included information women should know about taxes and insurance policies. Finally, for that time when women aged and their children left home, he created a course called Community Services. "Women need to know how to work for symphonies, art centers and museums," he said in a 1951 *Time* magazine article titled "For Happier Housewives." Rather than being paid for their work, they would volunteer their time and talents as

*During Professor Wright's term as the president of Smith College, the curriculum reflected his beliefs. The Smith students shown here are learning something about travel—how to gracefully place a suitcase in an overhead rack.*

upstanding community leaders. Other colleges across the country adopted similar home economics and parenting courses for their female students.

Margaret Clapp was also a professor who had recently become a college president. When appointed by all-female Wellesley College in Massachusetts, Clapp was one of only six female college presidents in the country. Her appointment, therefore, was news. Clapp disagreed with the new focus on family studies, she told a reporter from *Time*. A woman's place was anywhere she wanted to be. She might study medicine or law and work in a hospital or courtroom. But even if a woman chose the career of a housewife, her education should not differ from a man's. Women as well as men, she argued, "have the same functions as citizens, the same function as members of a community, the same functions as voters and volunteers."

The reporter described Margaret Clapp as having "deep brown eyes and dark wavy hair." She was slim and wore a bright red dress. She was, in fact, almost "too pretty" to be taken seriously, the reporter wrote. In other words, she was feminine. In writing about Benjamin Fletcher Wright, however, *Time* neglected to state the color of his eyes and hair. But that was the point. Wright was a man. Clapp was a woman. She had gotten the first A of 1950s femininity right—her appearance was attractive. But in regard to the other two, many men felt that her actions and her ambitions were somewhat aggressive!

More often than not, the popular media

*During Margaret Clapp's 1949–1966 term as president of Wellesley College, the institution's funding tripled, a wing was added to the library, and three new dormitories and a faculty club were constructed. Her real success lay in a curriculum that sent young women out into the world prepared for life beyond the household.*

*Debbie Reynolds and Bobby Van are shown in the 1953 movie* The Affairs of Dobie Gillis. *Typical of the 1950s, the female college students are portrayed as more interested in fun and romance than in academics.*

took Wright's side on the issues. Magazine advertisements and movies, in particular, suggested that a woman's desire for an education was really a masquerade. She might pretend to want a career, but secretly she was hoping to find a husband. Woodbury soap suggested the same idea in its magazine advertisement titled "Campus Sweetheart Weds." Bertha is the "sweetheart." The advertisement, drawn like a cartoon, shows Bertha riding a bike, washing her face, attending a formal dance and, in the final and largest image, wearing a wedding gown (rather than a graduation cap and gown). Although the advertisement says she is a college student, none of the images show her in class, reading, or even holding a book. Soap and a pretty complexion, not an education, will lead Bertha to her M.R.S. (Mrs.) degree.

In *The Affairs of Dobie Gillis*, a popular movie in 1953, Pansy Hammer goes to college to "work, work, work, learn, learn, learn."

It's her father's motto, not Pansy's. On her first day as a coed, she meets the fun-loving Dobie, who is also a college freshman. Dobie has no intention of working or learning. He has come to college to meet girls. Like Bertha, Pansy spends more time in rowboats and cars, smooching and singing with Dobie, than in class with her professors. When she does enter the chemistry laboratory, she mixes the wrong chemicals and causes a major explosion.

Bertha and Pansy were fictional coeds. But what did real-life female college students believe? Betty Friedan was determined to find out. Friedan was a college graduate who decided not to pursue her doctorate degree. Instead, she married and started a family. In the 1950s, as her children grew older, she began writing magazine articles about women's issues. She returned to Smith, the college from which she had graduated, to interview female students.

One young woman told Friedan that she had gone to college because her parents expected her to. "Everybody does," she said. "You're a social outcast at home if you don't." What if you wanted to continue your education? Friedan pressed. What if you wanted to earn your doctorate degree? It is what she herself had wanted to do. The young woman replied, "Everybody wants to graduate with a diamond ring. That's the important thing." Another student suggested that those women who were serious about their education often pretended they were not. Just as Jackie Bouvier had played dumb to attract boys (on her mother's advice), many female college students hid their true interests and ambitions.

Schools that promoted life studies and home economics courses

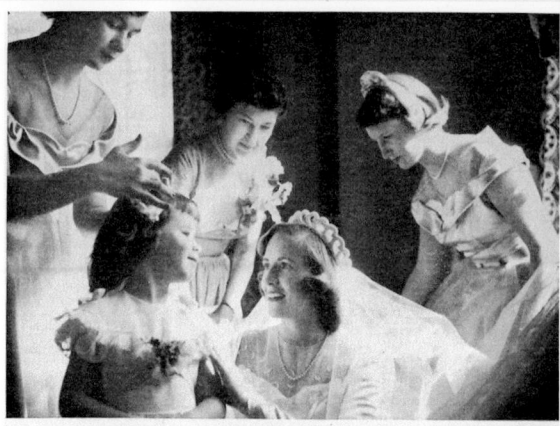

THE BRIDE...lovely Mrs. John Tristram Savage of Lawrence, Long Island. Her charming mother is Mrs. Augustus W. Bauer of Boston. The youngest enchantress is Susie Feltman. Note the soft, fresh, *young complexion* all three beauties share.

AT HER WEDDING...

three generations of beauty

MODEL, TV STAR Betty Savage knows *real* beauty comes from deep cleansing. Woodbury Soap contains a rich beauty-cream ingredient intended to help replace natural oils which are washed away.

SEE WHAT IT MEANS to have extra gentleness in a facial soap. See how bride-beautiful you can be. Buy Woodbury Soap today! Also in big beauty-bath size for *all-over* skin loveliness.

"I LOVE IT"! The bride freshens up. To Betty, the Woodbury beauty routine is a natural as breathing. Woodbury Soap may be used morning, noon, night—the more often, the more thrilling the results!

**Woodbury Facial Soap**...*with the Beauty-Cream Ingredient for the skin you love to touch*

*The early 1950s advertisements left no doubt about what the ultimate reward of using the proper soap would be—marriage!*

claimed they were helping women better adjust to the reality of their future lives. Betty Friedan didn't believe it. They were stunting women's growth, she said, preventing women from achieving their full potential. She didn't blame the colleges completely, though. "Millions of able women in this free land chose, themselves, not to use the door education could have opened for them," Friedan wrote.

It was up to women to demand better education and equal opportunities. To do so, however, meant challenging social stereotypes and sometimes even family traditions. Jade Snow Wong was one of seven children in a Chinese American family in San Francisco, California. Following Chinese culture, her father approved of his son's education but refused to send his daughter to college. Her future, he said, was to marry and

*Betty Friedan's interviews with Smith College students later formed the basis of her 1963 book* The Feminine Mystique. *In that book, she challenged the idea that women could only find fulfillment through marriage and motherhood.*

*Jade Snow Wong, shown here in 1953, inspired a generation of young women to express their independence. She also inspired the U.S. government. The State Department had her* Fifth Chinese Daughter *translated into forty languages to be distributed throughout the world as an example of life in a democracy.*

"*i can't help being born a girl,"* Wong wrote in bitterness. "*Perhaps I have a right to want more than sons. I am a person, besides being female!*"

—Jade Snow Wong, quoted in *Unbound Feet: A Social History of Chinese Women in San Francisco* (1995) by Judy Yung

raise sons. "I can't help being born a girl," she wrote in bitterness. "Perhaps I have a right to want more than sons. I am a person, besides being female!" Snow pursued her dream despite her father's objections. She graduated with honors from Mills College in California. She became a ceramic artist and a published author. Jade Snow challenged tradition. Her autobiography *Fifth Chinese Daughter*, published in 1950, would inspire a new generation of women to do the same.

## Beware the Other Woman!

Once a woman married and had children, the responsibility for making the marriage successful fell upon her shoulders, according to *Ladies' Home Journal*. In 1950 the magazine published the story of Henry and Ellen, a husband and wife with marital problems. A male marriage counselor who met with the young couple wrote the article.

Henry spoke first. His wife was wonderful, he told the marriage counselor. She was a good cook, a capable housekeeper, and a devoted churchgoer. But, he added, his marriage was "joyless." Ellen spoke next. Her marriage was "satisfactory," she said, but then she too added, "Maybe it's a little dull and uninspiring."

Henry and Ellen were in a marriage rut, the counselor told them. He suggested a few things they might do to improve the situation. First, he advised her to surprise her husband with an occasional token of affection—an unexpected kiss or a little gift from Woolworth's. (Woolworth was a chain of inexpensive five-and-dime stores.) Also, Ellen should respect her husband's privacy. "Don't disturb his belongings," the counselor said. "Don't open his wallet or read his mail without his approval. Don't read over his shoulder, either."

"Is that it?" Ellen asked.

"No, there's more." The counselor then suggested other things that Ellen might do—take an interest in her appearance, of course, but also show an interest in Henry's appearance, as well. She might compliment him on his hair or how handsome he is in that new shirt. Finally, she should appreciate Henry more. She could do this in simple ways, such as having his breakfast ready to be served to him in the morning.

# Queen of the Spiked Shoe

Wilma Rudolph wasn't just fast. She was lightning fast. She won three gold medals in track for the United States during the Summer Olympics in 1960. The news media lavished labels upon her, including "the fastest woman in the world," "the black pearl," and "the black gazelle." The *New York Times* crowned her "the queen of the spike shoe." In December 1960, news reporters from around the world voted her that year's International Athlete of the Year.

*When Wilma Rudolph returned from the 1960 Summer Olympics, the mayor of her hometown wanted to have a victory parade for her. Rudolph said she would not attend unless blacks and whites were able to go together. Her parade was the first integrated event in Clarksville, Tennessee.*

It was the first time a female athlete had ever won the title. In doing so, Wilma Rudolph had outscored champion boxer Floyd Patterson as well as a Russian weight lifter, a German sprinter, and an Australian marathon runner.

Enthusiastic fans stole her running shoes. Gentlemen began sending marriage proposals to the twenty-year-old college track star from Tennessee. Yes, she wanted to get married, she told reporters. Yes, she wanted to have children—preferably two girls. But first, she wanted to finish her college education. "A girl wants to be liked for herself, not just because she is fast," Rudolph stated.

When Wilma Rudolph was born—prematurely and weighing just 4.5 pounds (2 kilograms)—few people could have imagined her as the world's greatest female athlete. She was a sickly child. She came down with pneumonia, scarlet fever, and later polio, a disease that paralyzed her left leg. For years she wore a leg brace and special shoes. At the age of eleven, however, her brothers introduced her to basketball. She played hard against them. By the time she entered high school, she was a basketball star.

Rudolph did more than overcome physical disabilities, however. She impressed the press with her outstanding performances on the track, setting new records. In doing so, she inspired generations of female athletes to tie on their own spiked track shoes and run like the wind. Within a year of her impressive Olympic performance, Rudolph indeed marry. Unlike Maureen "Little Mo" Connolly, however, she did not toss away her track shoes or her goal of getting a college degree.

# "I Dreamed I Was Arrested . . ."

Each dream was different, but the bra was always a Maidenform. The manufacturer of Maidenform lingerie created the "I dreamed . . ." advertising campaign in 1949. The images were shocking for the time. Each showed a young, beautiful woman partially dressed. The "I dreamed I won the election in my Maidenform bra" ad portrayed a woman politician on stage amid voting banners and posters. She was wearing a full skirt that covered her legs. But instead of a blouse, she wore only a Maidenform bra.

For twenty years, Maidenform's "I dreamed . . ." campaign filled the pages of magazines. The images and the messages were female fantasies. Some dreams were geared toward women of high society, such as going to a masquerade ball or sailing to Europe. Others were dreams of achievement—being an artist or conducting an orchestra. Still others were dreams of the exotic—floating down the Nile River in Egypt or swirling a cape in a bullring as a toreador. At least one dream mocked women's intelligence. The "I dreamed I went to school" ad showed the Maidenform model adding two plus two and getting five. Some dreams put women in highly unlikely places, at least for the 1950s and 1960s—working at a building construction site and fighting a fire. What all the dreams had in common, aside from the usually conical-shaped bra, was an escape from the boredom of housewifery. Maidenform never ran an advertisement showing a mom dreaming of changing a dirty diaper or cleaning the bathtub in her glamorous bra.

*Maidenform had fun with its "I dreamed . . ." campaign. This ad not only has the usual elements of a woman in a bra in an unlikely situation but also adds a bit of humor in the play on the meaning of getting a lift.*

The "I dreamed . . ." campaign was so successful that *Mad* magazine ran a spoof in 1962. It stated, "I dreamed I was arrested for indecent exposure in my Maidenform bra."

By the late 1960s, women were no longer dreaming of these other lives and careers. They were living them. Perhaps that is why Maidenform dropped the dreams from its advertisements in 1969, although they would resurrect the campaign in 2005.

> *"Don't disturb his belongings.*
> *Don't open his wallet*
> *or read his mail without his approval.*
> *Don't read over his shoulder, either."*
>
> — Making Marriage Work, *Ladies' Home Journal,* 1950

These things could save her marriage.

And what was Henry to do to bring joy back into his marriage? Apparently nothing. The author had no specific suggestions for Henry.

Clifford R. Adams was the marriage counselor who wrote the article. In fact, his column, Making Marriage Work, appeared in every issue of *Ladies' Home Journal* throughout the decade. Each month the problem was somewhat different. It might be a husband who sulked or felt sorry for himself and didn't talk with his wife. Another month the troubling situation might be another woman to whom the husband was attracted. Again and again, Clifford R. Adams told the women who read this popular magazine the fault was theirs. "Some husbands don't get a chance to express themselves," he wrote, because "the wife is too talkative." Other men, he said, felt inferior. The wife's duty was to build the man's self-esteem by making him feel smart and important.

Printed across the cover of every issue of *Ladies' Home Journal* was this slogan: "The magazine women believe in." Did women believe what marriage counselor Adams told them each month? After reading his advice column in January 1950, did thousands of housewives suddenly surprise their husbands with unexpected trinkets from Woolworth's? Perhaps or perhaps not. Still the media message was clear. Marriage wasn't easy, but it was the woman's duty to try to make things better.

Short stories and novels also suggested that women were guilty of not doing enough to make their marriages happy. Take the story "Bitter Herb" by Nelia Gardner White, for example. "She was his wife and partner," the headline read, "but he couldn't live without the other woman." In these fictional romance stories, the "other woman" wasn't cooking three meals a day, changing diapers, and scrubbing the kitchen and bathroom floors in sloppy dungarees. Often she was one of those

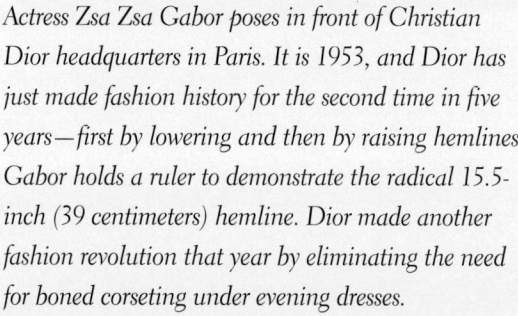

*Actress Zsa Zsa Gabor poses in front of Christian Dior headquarters in Paris. It is 1953, and Dior has just made fashion history for the second time in five years—first by lowering and then by raising hemlines. Gabor holds a ruler to demonstrate the radical 15.5-inch (39 centimeters) hemline. Dior made another fashion revolution that year by eliminating the need for boned corseting under evening dresses.*

*Perfume use expanded in the 1950s as cosmetic companies such as Yardley and Revlon released lower-priced fragrances to compete with those from designer fashion houses. The designers fought back, however, through advertising. The House of Dana, for example, called their scent Ambush. If the name didn't make it clear that the perfume was designed to catch a man, the spiderweb in the background erased all doubt.*

suspicious and single career women. She might be a neighbor or the wife's best friend. Whoever she was, she was always feminine. She dressed elegantly and wore velvety lipstick and spellbinding perfume. Her dress might be one of those "new look" designs by Christian Dior, with a cinched waist and full skirt that emphasized a woman's hips. The pages of fashion magazines were full of them. The cosmetics might be Hazel Bishop's "no smear lip-stick," which stayed on a woman's lips even after she had kissed a man. The perfume might be Ambush, which claimed to provide "romance in a bottle." One Ambush advertisement showed a beautiful woman in an evening gown. Behind her was a spider's web.

"Is your husband bored?" the magazines asked and then provided tips for how to avoid marriage monotony. A housewife might hang a small shelf or cabinet in the kitchen.

# Tiny Tears or Tog'l?

*The Tiny Tears doll could cry, drink, and even wet her diaper. The Tog'l set offered many possibilities for construction projects. The idea was that playtime for little girls was changing a diaper, while playtime for little boys was building a robot or a wagon.*

A children's jump rope rhyme of the twentieth century began like this: "First comes love, then comes marriage. . . ." What came next was a baby carriage. From 1946 through 1964, the United States experienced a baby boom. Millions of babies were born each year. As the infants grew into toddlers and the toddlers into adolescents, the "must have" items on Mom and Dad's shopping list included lots of toys, many of which were boy toys or girl toys.

Through play, children learn how to socialize. They also learn about who they are or may want to become. The toys of the 1950s reflected society's bias about women's roles.

Boys will play with trains and trucks, advised child-rearing expert Dr. Benjamin Spock, but girls will play with dolls, knowing that they are destined to become mothers. *Parents* magazine advised fathers to "rave over their (daughters') first attempts to bake a cake and make dresses for their dolls." An advertisement by the Mattel toy company suggested that girls dream of becoming a ballerina, but boys "were born to build and learn." That's why the company made Tog'l, a building block set, for boys and Tiny Tears for girls.

For somewhat older girls, there were board games such as Miss Popularity and Mystery Date. When playing "What Shall I Be?" girls competed by being the first to collect school, personality, and subject cards for a specific career. The players could choose from only six careers: teacher, actress, nurse, model, ballet dancer, or airline hostess (flight attendant). Missing from the game, however, were lawyers, physicians, and engineers—and all other male-dominated professions.

She could stock it with lipstick, comb, and perfume. This would put her "in the mood to meet any unexpected doorbell ringer." "Wear dresses!" advised Charles Contreras in his booklet *How to Fascinate Men.* "There's nothing cuddly about a woman wearing pants." Wear nail polish! Put lotion on your hands while vacuuming. Take a catnap during the day. If women did these simple, feminine things, then their husbands would hurry home from the office after work every day. The advice experts promised it would be so!

## Barbie's Closet

Ruth Handler, wife of one of the founders of the Mattel toy company, was watching her daughter Barbie play with paper dolls when she suddenly got an idea. As a mother, she knew Barbie loved dolls and clothes. She also understood that little girls like to act grown-up. What if, instead of manufacturing baby dolls for little girls, Mattel created a grown-up doll? Why not create a lifelike but miniature teenage fashion model?

Ruth Handler named her doll after her daughter. Barbie (the doll) came with a fully developed bosom, a tiny waist, and legs as long as a spider's (but more shapely). She had a long ponytail, a black-and-white-striped strapless bathing suit, and open-toe high heel shoes made of plastic. To accommodate the heels, Barbie's tiny plastic feet were constantly standing on tiptoes. The idea of a skinny teenage doll was controversial. Dolls in the 1950s were usually cuddly babies, not adults. Barbie wasn't great for hugging, Ruth Handler admitted, but she was perfect for dressing.

Barbie made her debut at a toy fair in 1959, selling for three dollars. Sales were slow at first, but by summer, the doll had caught on. To Mattel's surprise, the company sold more than 350,000 Barbies the first year. A cultural icon had been born.

*The Barbie doll was released in 1959. Until then, the only adult-figured dolls were two-dimensional paper dolls. The original Barbie sold for three dollars but has sold to recent collectors for as much as ten thousand dollars.*

Soon Barbie came with all sorts of elegantly designed costumes, most with accessories such as a change of shoes, a hat, and a purse. Barbie's outfits defined who she was. Dress her in her tutu and she was a ballerina. She had a tennis outfit, pajamas for slumber parties, lingerie, and a wedding gown. She did not have, at least not in the 1950s and early 1960s, a space suit to be an astronaut or a lab coat and stethoscope to be a doctor.

Barbie was a phenomenal success, earning millions for Mattel. Her appeal wasn't just her painted sky blue eyes or blonde ponytail. It was her wardrobe. No one bought just a doll. Parents came back again and again to purchase new outfits for Barbie. Mattel described this consumer strategy as "the razor and the razor blade" technique. Said a company spokesperson, "You get hooked on one and you have to buy the other."

In 1961 Mattel followed society's expectations for young women in suburban neighborhoods. They created a boyfriend for Barbie (named Ken after Ruth Handler's son). According to Mattel legend, Barbie met Ken while making a television commercial in 1961. Barbie's dream house and a few cars soon followed. At some point, Mattel wanted Barbie to marry and have children, but Ruth Handler objected. Marriage and motherhood would significantly change Barbie's image. The doll's popularity was rooted in her image as a glamorous teenage model. Barbie, therefore, would never age and never have children. She did, however, have a younger sister, a doll Mattel christened Skipper.

*Barbie was originally a blonde teenage model. She became a college student in 1964. As women became more prominent in the workplace, Barbie kept pace with more than eighty careers, ranging from astronaut to basketball star, paleontologist to rock star. She could also be a brunette as well as black or Hispanic.*

Producing the various Barbie models and outfits took a team of talented individuals, many of them women working in the fashion industry. Ruth Handler hired fashion designer Charlotte Johnson to create the doll's wardrobe. Since Barbie was a fashion model in the early 1960s, Johnson got many of her design ideas from fashion shows in Paris and even from popular movies. She and her team created chic miniclothes—an evening gown with a pink chiffon scarf, a brocade coat with fur trim on the sleeves, and a red linen suit. They came with accessories—matching shoes, handbags, and often jewelry. The zippers worked. The coats were lined. Such attention to detail, as well as the designs themselves, made Barbie a very glamorous young woman. Barbie even had her own hair stylist. Jean Ann Burger created wigs for the plastic-sculpted doll. Hiroe Okubo-Wulf became Barbie's face painter, altering the doll's lips, eyes, and overall expression to give her a more up-to-date look.

As women's roles began to change during the 1960s, Barbie's interests and activities also changed. Barbie became a nurse in 1961, a student teacher in 1965, and a surgeon in 1973. (In the 1980s, the clothes in Barbie's closet changed even more dramatically. She gained tennis outfits and basketball uniforms. Her wardrobe grew to include the clothes of a cowgirl, a firefighter, a police officer, an airplane pilot, and a soldier.

*"Playing Barbie" meant that girls were no longer limited to pretending to be a mother.*

Barbie even ran for president—but not until the year 2000.)

Not everyone loved the teenage doll. Some women charged that Barbie reinforced feminine stereotypes. Barbie was big-busted and blonde, a doll version of a Hollywood "bombshell." Author Linda Scott remembers her mother telling her that Barbie "was not the kind of woman that nice little girls grew up to be." Others criticized Mattel for promoting thinness as an ideal beauty type through Barbie's too-tiny waist, too-large breasts, and too-long legs. Despite the criticisms, Barbie continued to be popular. "Playing Barbie" became a different social experience for girls of the late 1960s. They were no longer limited to pretending to be a mother. Rather, they could be Barbie the model or Barbie the nurse or eventually Barbie the veterinarian, surgeon, astronaut, or athlete. And that, said Ruth Handler, was the secret to Barbie's success.

# Nearly Me

Ruth Handler was a business success story of the 1950s and 1960s. She became president of Mattel in 1967. In 1970 Ruth Handler received upsetting news. Doctors had discovered cancer in her breast. To treat the cancer, doctors surgically removed her breast, an operation called a mastectomy. To lose such an intimate part of her body can change the way a woman feels about herself. Like many other women who lose a breast, Ruth Handler no longer felt whole. The operation had left scars on her chest. Deep inside, she was emotionally hurt as well. At that time, the available prosthetics, or artificial breasts, were not lifelike or comfortable.

Instead of giving in to hopelessness, Ruth Handler began working on a new plastic invention—not a doll this time but a breast replacement. Her invention had the weight and shape of a natural breast and was comfortable to wear. The woman who had created the first doll with breasts called her breast replacement for real women Nearly Me.

Ruth Handler's two inventions served different functions. Barbie was a toy. Nearly Me was a medical prosthetic. The two products, however, share something in common: a woman's self-esteem. "When I conceived Barbie, I believed it was important to a little girl's self-esteem to play with a doll that has breasts," said Ruth Handler. "Now I find it even more important to return that self-esteem to women who have lost theirs."

*Although Barbie was her biggest commercial success, Ruth Handler took equal pride in her development of prosthetic breasts for mastectomy patients. She is shown here in 1977 demonstrating the product in her storage room.*

*Audrey Hepburn's slim boyish figure, close-cropped hairdo, and simple wardrobe was a big change for the U.S. fashion scene. She is shown here as she appeared in the 1954 film* Sabrina.

## The Gamine Beauty

"Audrey Hepburn has enormous heron's eyes and dark eyebrows slanted towards the Far East. Her facial features show character rather than prettiness. . . . Her mouth is wide, with a cleft under the lower lip too deep for classical beauty," wrote photographer Cecil Beaton in *Vogue* in 1954. Hepburn's was a different kind of beauty. She was childlike, said some in the media. She was gamine, wrote others, which is another way of saying charmingly tomboyish. "Nobody ever looked like her before World War II," wrote Beaton.

Suddenly the United States had a new feminine ideal. She was tall with a long neck, willowy, and rather flat chested. She was spirited and spunky rather than submissive. "She changed the way men looked at women—and, more important, the way women looked at themselves," wrote a journalist in *Newsweek*.

Her films *Roman Holiday* and *Sabrina* made Audrey Hepburn a Hollywood star in the early 1950s. At the time, Hollywood's ideal woman was more often than not blonde, buxom, and curvy hipped. Betty Grable, Marilyn Monroe, and Lana Turner were actresses whose figures fit that hourglass ideal. Then there were the innocent girl-next-door types portrayed in the 1950s and 1960s by actresses such as Debbie Reynolds and Doris Day. But Audrey Hepburn didn't fit either of these Hollywood ideas—in fact, she wasn't a type at all. In front of the camera, said director William Wyler, she simply became "Miss Audrey Hepburn." Wyler called that special something on the screen "element X." But even he couldn't quite explain what X was, just that Audrey Hepburn had it.

"Less is more" was Hepburn's fashion philosophy, said her son Sean Ferrer. Her choice

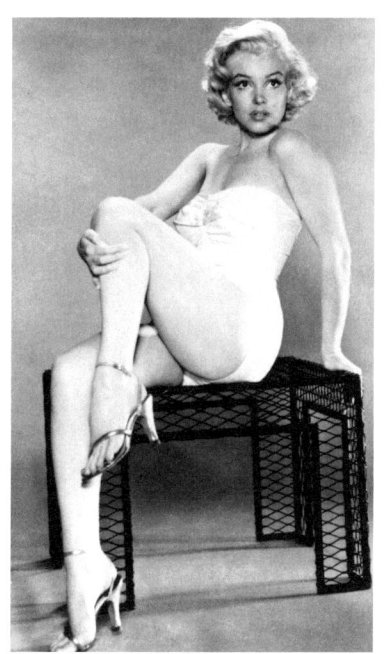

*Audrey Hepburn's appeal was the opposite of the glamour queens of the mid-1950s. Betty Grable (top left), Marilyn Monroe (lower left), and Lana Turner (top right) were all huge box office draws. They were blonde and curvaceous, with enormous sex appeal.*

of clothing usually included simple, straight lines. She often dressed in tight-fitting black pants and flat shoes. (Her feet, like Jacqueline Bouvier's, were large. Hepburn wore a size 10.) Her dark hair was often cut short, pixie-style. Anyone could look like her, she once told an interviewer. All they had to do was buy a little sleeveless black dress. Across the United States, women did. They imitated her style, from her pixie haircut to her low heel shoes.

Hepburn did not think of herself as beautiful. Her own mother once called her an ugly duckling, she said. Her beauty, said her son, came from inside. She was a kind, caring person who loved children. After she became a mother, she brought her sons with her while making films so she could be close to them. As they grew older and started school, she made a decision. She said, "I had to make a choice in my life of missing films or missing my children. It was a very easy decision to make." She gave up the films.

Audrey Hepburn was an icon of popular culture, a role model to many women. She possessed the three A's of femininity: appearance, actions, and ambition. She just interpreted them in her own unique way.

# Three Film Stereotypes . . .

Hollywood movies are entertainment. They provide escape from the everyday world and something else too: image. In films from the 1950s and 1960s, female characters often projected one of three images.

*The Glamorous Woman.* She's fashion conscious and socially sophisticated. If a blonde, she might also be a little dumb. In 1953's *How to Marry a Millionaire*, three glamorous fashion models plot to snare wealthy men into proposing marriage. All three models fall in love, and money becomes unimportant after all. Glamorous women could also be downright villainous.

*The Virtuous Woman.* She's moral, innocent, and usually pretty smart. She's sometimes not as beautiful as the glamorous woman (at least, not at first). In 1957's *Funny Face*, Audrey Hepburn plays a virtuous, plain-Jane bookworm. When a fashion photographer discovers her, the bookworm emerges from her cocoon as a beautiful butterfly.

*Doris Day, shown here with Rock Hudson in* Pillow Talk *(1959), a role for which she won a best actress Oscar nomination. Day's roles as the virtuous, good-hearted woman made her top box office in the early 1960s. By the late 1960s, the sexual revolution was under way, and the public's tastes changed. Comics made fun of Day as the world's oldest virgin, and her ratings dropped.*

*The Almost-Independent Woman.* Doris Day was the queen of the movie box office in the early 1960s. Her characters were often the same type: a successful, attractive, and single career woman who isn't quite as smart when it comes to matters of the heart. By movie's end, the Doris Day character finds true love and gives up her single, independent life. At least that's what usually happened in 1950s and 1960s movies.

# ...and Two Unique Authors

In the small town of Gilmanton, New Hampshire, Grace Metalious was married to a schoolteacher. He didn't much approve of his wife's literary aspirations—or her sloppy housekeeping. In 1956 she sent her novel off to a literary agent in the hope that it might earn her some much-needed cash.

That same year in New York City, Nelle Harper Lee was also having a hard time making ends meet. She worked as a reservations clerk for an airline. Then at Christmas, two friends gave Lee a remarkable gift—a check that would allow her to quit her job so that she could write full-time for a year.

The books Grace Metalious and Harper Lee would publish within a few years of each other would be significantly different in subject matter and writing style. Each would rock the publishing world.

Grace Metalious set her novel in a small New England town she called Peyton Place. She wrote about the emotional longings—and explicit sexual experiences—of a widowed mother raising her daughter alone. Published in September 1956, *Peyton Place* became an overnight sensation. Although reviewers criticized it as scandalous and poorly written, the novel soared to the top of the best-seller list—earning Metalious a great deal of money.

Harper Lee also set her novel in a small town, the fictional Maycomb, Alabama. She wrote about a young girl's relationship with her father, an attorney named Atticus Finch. When Finch defends a black man accused of raping a white woman, the little girl learns the meaning of racism and intolerance. But she learns, too, about love. Published in 1960, *To Kill a Mockingbird* also became a best seller. A year later, the novel earned one of literature's highest awards, the Pulitzer Prize. The ensuing attention confused and at times angered Lee. She shunned fame and returned to her hometown to live quietly alone, never to publish another book.

These two authors wrote very different books about life in small town America, but each book had a major impact. *Peyton Place* was a "breakthrough for freedom of expression," said Emily Toth, who later wrote a biography of Grace Metalious. "It (*Peyton Place*) set new parameter for what you could say in a book—especially about women." *To Kill a Mockingbird*'s theme of social justice introduced millions of mainstream Americans to civil rights issues.

# chapter two

# Mrs. TV Consumer

*A housewife in her 1950s kitchen*

"The function of daytime TV . . . is neither to entertain nor to instruct. It is to provide a pleasant background babble—rather like an indoor waterfall—while the American housewife goes about her chores."

—Dan Sullivan, *New York Times*, 1967

# During World War II, U.S. industries

shifted their production from consumer goods to war goods. Instead of building automobiles, Ford built army jeeps. Instead of vacuum cleaners, Hoover produced parachutes, life-belt inflating devices, and motors for bomber propellers. Instead of refrigerators, Westinghouse manufactured torpedoes. Once the war ended, U.S. industries were eager to shift back to the consumer market. And the American housewife was on top on their consumer list.

In the new self-service supermarkets of the 1950s, housewives filled their shopping carts with the latest prepackaged and ready-to-eat food items: boxed cake mixes, packaged sliced cheese, canned onion soup, quick Minute Rice, presweetened cereal and, in 1954, the United States' latest food fad, the frozen TV dinner. Turkey and dressing came in a foil-wrapped package that could be quickly popped in the oven and cooked. A 1950s magazine advertisement for Swanson's frozen TV dinners showed a young woman in gloves and hat in her kitchen, looking at her wristwatch. "I'm late,"

she says, "but dinner won't be." She's late because she was shopping. Her new hatbox is on the kitchen table.

Manufacturers improved old products. Any appliance purchased before the war was simply out of date. The new electric stoves cooked more efficiently. The new refrigerators had larger freezers to accommodate frozen TV dinners. In the 1950s, housework became glamorous. Manufacturers created new colors for their appliances with the hope of persuading women to turn in their plain old white

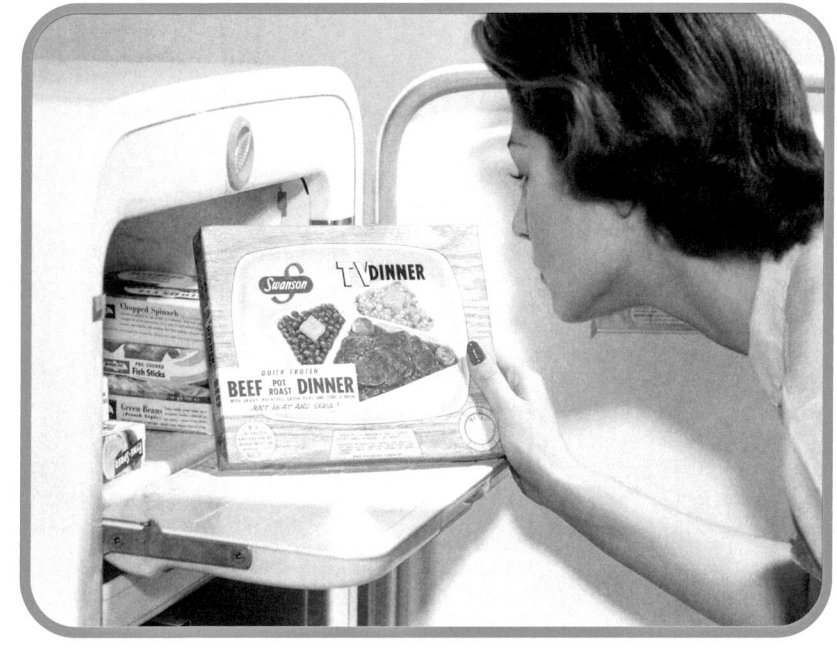

*This housewife's freezer holds frozen fish sticks and frozen chopped spinach—both fairly new inventions. But the supreme timesaver of the 1950s was the Swanson TV Dinner. The ability to have a full meal "piping ready in twenty-five minutes or less" was an incredible concept in pre-microwave days.*

ones for something more exciting . . . in turquoise or pink, perhaps. "Never has a whole people spent so much money on so many expensive things . . . as Americans are doing today," reported *Fortune* magazine.

And a new advertising medium—television—helped create a whirlwind shopping spree. Americans bought as many as seven million television sets each year during the 1950s. But television was a medium for more than entertainment. Moving images offered a new way to sell products to millions of American families. In the daytime, in particular, women were the predominant television viewers. "It was a salesman's dream," wrote historian David Halberstam.

## The Femcees

Westinghouse hired a thirty-three-year-old actress named Betty Furness to demonstrate its kitchen appliances on televised commercials. Furness performed these demonstrations live in front of the camera. Any mistake she might make, either speaking her lines or demonstrating the product, could not be erased or shot over. The commercials were also long. They ran from one and a half to three minutes.

*Television was a new technology in the 1950s. TV ads offered a huge array of products from which to choose.*

Furness could have read her lines off cue cards, or large poster boards held up behind the camera. Instead she memorized them. She understood that television was different from movies. Movies played in theaters, but television played in people's living rooms.

That television was more personal was partly the power of its persuasion. "I wanted to look into the eye of the camera, therefore the eye of the viewer," she said.

Betty Furness became known as the lady from Westinghouse. She had blonde, curly hair and a broad smile. She purchased her own fashionable wardrobe to wear during the commercials. That way, she said, she could dress the way women wished they could, instead of the way Westinghouse's male executives thought a housewife should dress. Instead of cotton print housedresses, Furness wore stylish dresses with narrow waists and full skirts, high heel shoes, and even pearl necklaces. Furness wasn't a housewife or a mother, but that was her appeal, she believed. Westinghouse executives asked her to wear a wedding ring and an apron so she would look more like the famous radio cooking show hostess Betty Crocker. She refused. She wasn't Betty Crocker, she told them. She was Betty Furness.

Her instincts to appear fashionable rather than ordinary won her fame. Women liked her glamorous style. When she opened the refrigerator door, female viewers were paying as much attention to her dress as to the spacious shelves inside the appliance. Furness ended each commercial with this simple statement: "You can be sure if it's Westinghouse." The American television

*Television spokesperson Betty Furness talks directly to the camera about the latest 1952 Westinghouse washer and dryer models. Furness made headlines when she spent a total of three thousand dollars on twenty-eight new outfits to wear for her Westinghouse commercials. She later had a government job as assistant for consumer affairs, a post she held until 1969.*

public was sure of her. Sales of Westinghouse appliances soared.

As the Westinghouse spokeswoman, Furness was among television's first female personalities. A femcee, as the TV industry referred to these women, could earn a lofty salary—from $50,000 to $150,000 per year. She had to be sophisticated but not smug.

# The Housewife's "Troubles and Bubbles"…

Each program began the same way. Master of ceremonies Jack Bailey stood onstage and bellowed into his microphone, "Do YOU want to be… queen for a day?" From the television studio audience of mostly middle-aged women came a thunderous reply: "YES!" *Queen for a Day* was a popular television program of the 1950s and 1960s. Women chosen from the studio audience competed for prizes, often household appliances or clothing. To win, each woman told a true but sad story about her life. Her husband might be ill and out of work, and she is unable to pay the next month's rent. Or she might be a widow who has to raise her children herself. Jack Bailey interviewed each contestant on camera, pumping her for more details. He kept tissues nearby and even smelling salts should the distraught contestant faint from the stress of publicly admitting her hardships. The more sorry her story and the more tears she wept, the more likely the studio audience would vote her queen. They voted for each woman, one at a time, by applauding. An "applause meter" measured the volume of their clapping hands.

*Time* magazine called the program a mixture of "troubles and bubbles" but admitted it was very popular. Approximately ten million people, or half of the nation's television viewers, tuned in faithfully to be assured that in the United States, anyone could live the good life—if only for a day.

*Queen for a Day was an early version of television's popular reality show. A woman would tell her life story, and the audience would vote via an applause meter. Then, to the strains of the studio orchestra playing "Pomp and Circumstance," the winning contestant would be draped with a red velvet, fur-trimmed cape and crowned Queen for a Day. This winner, shown here with host Jack Bailey in a 1958 episode, is a fifteen-year-old mother and widow.*

# ...And Welcome to Sudsville

Joanne Barron's life was full of ups but mostly downs. Her husband had died leaving her a widow with a young child. Her mother-in-law was downright bossy and would like nothing better than to take her granddaughter away from Joanne to raise in her own way in her own home. For fifteen minutes each weekday afternoon, housewives tuned their television sets to *Search for Tomorrow* to watch Joanne try to overcome her bad luck.

*Search for Tomorrow* was a daytime television drama that first aired on September 3, 1951. Because the show's sponsors were Joy and Spic and Span (two household cleaning products), the melodramatic daytime show was labeled a "soap opera." Other soap operas captured the hearts of housewives, too, in the 1950s, including *As the World Turns, Secret Storm,* and *The Guiding Light.* In each soap opera, female characters struggle with daunting challenges, including bankruptcy, ill health, and murder (in addition to domineering relatives and unfaithful husbands).

Afternoon soap operas were not a television invention of the 1950s. Radio had broadcast serialized stories of characters and their conflicts in the 1930s and 1940s. But television soap operas were different. They were visual. The TV camera took viewers inside the characters' kitchens and living rooms. As a result, many housewives felt as if Joanne Barron and all the other soap opera characters were their friends. Women scheduled their days so that they would be available to watch their favorite shows.

While many people derided soap operas as silly and sentimental, others saw the powerful influence the shows' story lines could have on its viewers. In the mid-1960s, a female character named Bert on *The Guiding Light* discovers she has cancer. Female audiences did more than hope for Bert's recovery. Bert's condition increased awareness of a particular type of cancer and a test that could detect the cancer early and so save lives—the Pap smear. The show's writers received letters from women who had said Bert's strength had given them the courage to confront their medical problems, as well.

By the 1970s, ratings for daytime soap operas had slipped somewhat. Still, the genre remained popular into the twenty-first century.

She had to be beautiful but not boastful. Otherwise, she might alienate her female viewers. In addition to radiating personality, a femcee had to sell products. When she wasn't demonstrating a kitchen appliance, as Furness did in commercials, a femcee often hosted game shows, where the prizes were wonderful new consumer goods on display in department stores and on supermarket shelves.

The Big Payoff was one of the longest-running game shows of the 1950s, running from 1951 until 1959. The femcee was the former Miss America of 1945, Bess Myerson. She was 5 feet 10 inches (178 cm) tall with long brunette hair. Her beauty, however, was not the only reason she got the job.

Myerson was Jewish. When she entered the Miss America Pageant, the officials encouraged her to change her recognizably Jewish last name to Merrick so that the judges wouldn't be prejudiced against her. But she refused to hide her religion. After winning the crown, however, the pageant's sponsors would not allow a Jewish beauty queen to pose with and, thereby, endorse their products. She did not pose in Catalina swimsuits as other Miss Americas had. Nor did she pose with Ford automobiles. She began speaking out against prejudice. "You cannot be beautiful and hate," she said during one of her appearances. "Miss America represents all America. It makes no difference who she is or who her parents are. Side by side, Catholic, Protestant, and Jew stand together." During one of Myerson's public appearances,

*Bess Myerson* (far right) *and her cohost Randy Merriman* (far left) *pose during a 1953 segment of* The Big Payoff. *In the show, a steelworker and his telephone company employee wife* (above) *won two round-trip tickets to anywhere in Europe. The wife also won a new wardrobe, including the mink coat she is modeling.*

television producer Walt Farmer heard her. Her ability to speak out against prejudice with dignity impressed him. Television should reflect the country's diversity, he believed, and he hired her.

Although Catalina swimsuits and the Ford Motor Company had not allowed a Jewish woman to promote their products in 1945, the television sponsors of 1951 seemingly had no such prejudice. Bess Myerson,

> ## "Miss America represents all America. It makes no difference who she is or who her parents are. Side by side, Catholic, Protestant, and Jew stand together."
>
> — Bess Myerson, Miss America 1945

often dressed in an evening gown, began each episode of *The Big Payoff* showcasing the extravagant array of products that contestants could win — everything from luggage to lingerie. The grand prizes were a trip to Paris, cash, and a mink coat, which Myerson

modeled on every show. The contestants were husbands. Each contestant's wife also appeared on the show, but she didn't speak much. First, the husband explained why his wife deserved to win the glamorous items. On one show, an airline pilot said that he and his wife had been married for twenty-four years, but she still didn't have a home of her own. Another contestant said there wasn't enough money in the household budget to buy his wife beautiful things. Next came the contest questions. For each question the husband answered correctly, he could select a prize. If he answered all questions correctly, he got "the big payoff."

## TV's Humorous Housewives

Television promoted consumerism, and it also promoted an idealized image of the American family. In situation comedies and in daytime soap operas, actresses portrayed housewives and mothers. The characters Margaret Anderson on *Father Knows Best*, Harriet Nelson on *The Adventures of Ozzie and Harriet*, and June Cleaver on *Leave It to Beaver* lived in single-family homes in suburban neighborhoods. These TV housewives and mothers were lovingly strict but tolerant with their children. Brothers and sisters might argue and call one another squirt and sissy, but by the end of the show, they always made

up. Mom stayed home and cooked hot breakfasts and dusted the furniture, usually wearing a dress. Neither she nor her TV husband swore, drank liquor, or slapped each other around. If a plate shattered, it was because someone was gee-whiz clumsy rather than gosh-darn angry while drying the dishes.

*I Love Lucy*, starring actress Lucille Ball, was different from the other comedy shows.

*Counterclockwise from upper left, scenes from* The Adventures of Ozzie and Harriet, Father Knows Best, *and* Leave It to Beaver *reflect an idealized view of families. A beautifully dressed, well-made-up TV mother always did her housework in a pretty dress and high heels.*

# Bad Reviews for Beulah

*Beulah* was the first television series to feature an African American in the leading role. During the show's first two years, African American actress Ethel Waters portrayed Beulah, a maid to the Henderson family. In 1951 actress Hattie McDaniel replaced Waters in the role. Soon after, an illness forced Hattie McDaniel to leave the show. Louise Beavers, a third African American actress, stepped in front of the television camera.

Beulah was sassy but wise. Although just a maid, she was the one who solved the Hendersons' weekly crises. The show was "kitchen comedy," since most of the action—and the laughs—took place in the kitchen. But it wasn't Beulah's kitchen. It was the Hendersons'. Nothing in the house belonged to Beulah. The year the television show first went on the air, approximately 60 percent of working black women held jobs as housekeepers. But that didn't make the show realistic or right, said the National Association for the Advancement of Colored People (NAACP). The NAACP denounced the show at its annual meeting in 1951. *Beulah* depicted black people in a demeaning and stereotypical way, the organization said, suggesting they were "inferior, lazy, dumb and dishonest."

*Beulah* went off the air in 1953. Fifteen years would pass before another African American actress would star in a television program. The actress was Diahann Carroll, and the show was *Julia.* Carroll portrayed a single mom who was also a nurse.

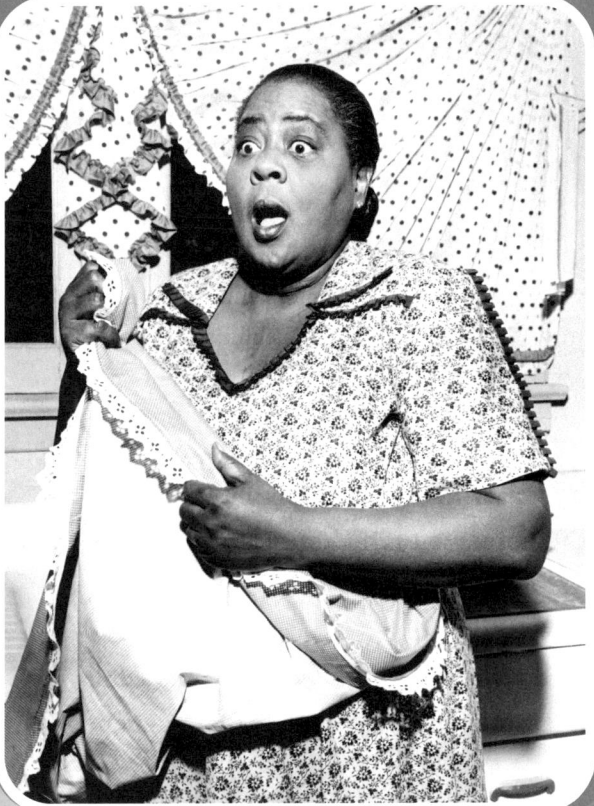

*Louise Beavers (left) was one of three actresses to portray the title character in the television show Beulah. Beavers was aware that the role was stereotyped, but she agreed with Hattie McDaniel, her predecessor in the role. McDaniel once said, "I can be a maid for $7 a week or I can play a maid for $700 a week."*

*Lucille Ball* (right) *of* I Love Lucy *delighted audiences by being the not-so-perfect housewife—in fact, she was far from it! She is shown here with her friend Ethel Mertz (Vivian Vance) in a 1952 episode in which the two of them shove chocolates into their mouths and into their clothing as they try to keep up with a conveyor belt in a candy factory.*

Ball played Lucy Ricardo. Lucy's real-life husband, Cuban-born bandleader Desi Arnaz, played her TV husband as well. Instead of living in a suburban home with children, the Ricardos lived in a city apartment owned by their friends, Fred and Ethel Mertz. Lucy was a housewife like Margaret Anderson and June Cleaver, but she had little else in common with those happy-to-stay-at-home moms. Lucy desperately wanted to escape the doldrums of her apartment. She dreamed of being a celebrity. Each week she hatched a new scheme in her quest for fame and fortune, usually talking Ethel into joining her. Lucy usually failed in very funny ways. By the end of the program, Ricky always forgave his wife for her crazy antics. And Lucy promised

to settle down and be a happy housewife. Until the next week's episode.

*I Love Lucy* was a tremendous success. So many viewers stayed home to watch Lucy's antics—an estimated 30 million people—that one New York City department store decided to close its doors early on Monday nights rather than compete with the show. When *I Love Lucy* played on TV, consumers stayed home to laugh rather than shop.

The real-life Lucy was no clown. With Desi Arnaz, Ball formed her own television production company called Desilu Productions. In an industry run mostly by men, she had a reputation as a tough businesswoman. She was a demanding boss, said Madelyn Pugh, one of the writers. "She would get impatient when things weren't working or impatient that people were phony or weren't doing their jobs," said Pugh. "She was usually right, but she scared everybody." Americans didn't see that side of Ball, however. They loved her for her screwball ways. Like TV's other humorous housewives, Lucy wasn't a very realistic portrayal of real American women. After all, how many women will disguise themselves with a fake nose to meet a movie star and then accidentally set the nose on fire? Instead of trying to be realistic, *I Love Lucy* exaggerated and made fun of the quirks and shortcomings of a married couple.

## Mothers of Invention

Television's daytime viewers were predominantly stay-at-home housewives and mothers. The television sponsors of daytime programs were often manufacturers of the products women used. Among the sponsors for the daytime *Garry Moore Show*, for example, were Kellogg cereal, Duff's Baking Mix, and Stokely-Van Camp canned foods. Moore's daytime show featured a variety of acts, including comedy and musical performances. He also hosted an evening game show, but *Time* magazine reported, "His heart belongs to his housewives." During the day, the house is empty. The husband is at work. The children are at school, and housewives, said Moore, get lonely. "I'm convinced they want to hear the sounds of merriment while they work."

Of course, not all housewives watched TV during the day. Some were inventing consumer products of their own. Take Lillian Menasche Hochberg, for example. She was alone during the day, but she wasn't so much lonely as she was worried about her weekly budget. (Her husband was a hat maker who earned seventy-five dollars a week managing one of his family's stores.) Once she became pregnant with her first child in 1951, she realized that she'd need more money to care for her growing family. "A working wife was an embarrassing commentary on her husband's earning power," she said, referring to the attitude of the time that if a wife worked outside the home, it was because her husband was unable to support her. "I had to earn money, but I couldn't leave the house."

And so, using two thousand dollars in wedding gift money, she took a risk on starting a home business. The mother-to-be purchased a supply of leather handbags and belts and placed an advertisement in an issue of *Seventeen* magazine. It wasn't a very large advertisement, but something in the headline "Be the first to sport that personalized look on your bag and belt" caught the eyes of the young women who read the magazine. Three months later, she had received thirty-two thousand dollars in orders for her monogrammed leather goods. She had not expected such a response. Nor had her husband. He viewed her at-home business as a hobby, even though she was proud of her accomplishment and viewed it as a real business. She told no one in her community what she was doing in her kitchen during the day. "I was a closet worker," she would later admit to a reporter from *Working Woman* magazine. "Nobody knew for years that I had a job."

By 1956 the business shifted from magazine advertisements to a sixteen-page catalog of gift items and other knickknacks (decorative ornaments for the house). It was renamed Lillian Vernon, using Lillian's first name and the name of the town out of which she worked, Mount Vernon, New York.

*Lillian Vernon* (front) *is shown shopping in Hong Kong for unique products to offer in her catalog. Begun in the kitchen of her apartment in 1951, her company has grown to employ more than thirty-five hundred people and to ship nearly five million packages a year.*

## "I was a closet worker. Nobody knew for years that I had a job."

—Lillian Hochberg, recalling her early career to a reporter from *Working Woman* magazine, 1986

# The Kitchen Debate

Consumerism wasn't just a television advertising strategy. It was a political strategy as well. In 1959 Vice President Richard Nixon traveled to the Soviet Union. He met with the nation's premier and leader of the Communist Party, Nikita Khrushchev. The two world leaders held a debate, but they did not speak about atomic bombs. Instead, they argued about kitchens! Actually, the argument compared the Soviet versus the American way of life.

Nixon believed that every country in the world—or at least the Soviet Union—held the same attitude toward women as the United States did. "What we want is to make easier the life of our housewives," Nixon stated. The modern appliances Westinghouse and other U.S. manufacturers produced did just that. In the United States, he boasted, successful men have attractive wives and comfortable homes in suburban neighborhoods with grassy parks and good schools.

"Don't you have a machine that puts food in to the mouth and pushes it down?" asked the Soviet leader. His remark was satirical, suggesting that Americans were soft and lazy. Then it was Khrushchev's turn to boast. Soviet women were not expected to be full-time housewives. They worked just as men did.

In the United States, Nixon said, men and women have the right to choose how and where they will live. Most ordinary Americans could save their wages and buy a new six-room ranch home.

Khrushchev countered, "All you have to do to get a house is to be born in the Soviet Union."

Neither leader convinced the other of his point of view. The media labeled this biting exchange the Kitchen Debate. The argument wasn't really over kitchens or appliances. It wasn't even about women. The debate illustrated the differences in the political thinking of the two leaders and their countries.

*Soviet premier Nikita Khrushchev (center) laughs with U.S vice president Richard Nixon (right) during a tour of the American technology trade exhibit in Moscow, July 1959. The exhibit inspired what was to be known as the Kitchen Debate. It took place in the kitchen area of a model house exhibit. Nixon pushed to steer the conversation away from weapons and toward his country's strength in producing household appliances.*

When *Working Women* interviewed her in 1986, this stay-at-home mother and entrepreneur had grown her home-based business into one of the United States' most successful direct-mail businesses, worth millions of dollars. So well known was her company that she eventually changed her own name legally to "Lillian Vernon." Her business would continue to grow and become one of the leading mail-order gift catalogs of the early twenty-first century.

Other women also became successful producers of consumer goods in the 1950s and 1960s. Many used their homes as laboratories for their innovations. Bette Clair McMurray dropped out of high school to marry a man named Nesmith. She later went to night school to get her high school diploma. During the day, she worked as a secretary for the chairperson of a Texas bank. In the evenings, she enjoyed her hobby—painting and drawing. Her knowledge of paints, which she had taught herself, was to help her solve a messy problem at work.

Whenever McMurray made a typing error at work, she had to erase the mistake. But typewriter ribbon ink was made of carbon and often smeared the paper. When that happened, McMurray had to start the job all over again. In her kitchen, she experimented with adding a touch of color to tint water-based paint the same shade as the bank stationery.

*In 1966 Bette McMurray's business began by her producing a few bottles of her typewriter correction fluid in her kitchen. By 1975 she was the head of the Liquid Paper corporation, producing 25 million bottles a year.*

She used the mixture at work to paint over a typing error, rather than erasing it. When the paint dried, she could type over it. When the other secretaries began asking for bottles of their own paint, McMurray's kitchen-sink business began. She called her product Mistake Out. Eventually, she changed the name to Liquid Paper. It took her a few years, but by 1967, McMurray had become a millionaire, the inventor of one of the most practical office supplies of the late twentieth century.

Meanwhile, Marion Donovan was experimenting with her plastic bathroom shower curtain. She was plenty tired of washing dirty diapers. The diapers often leaked, and then she'd have to wash the crib sheets and some-times the blankets too. She fashioned a diaper cover from the plastic curtain and created the first disposable diaper. When no manufacturing company was interested, she started her own business. She later sold her company to the Keko Corporation. In 1961 the disposable diaper became known worldwide as Pampers.

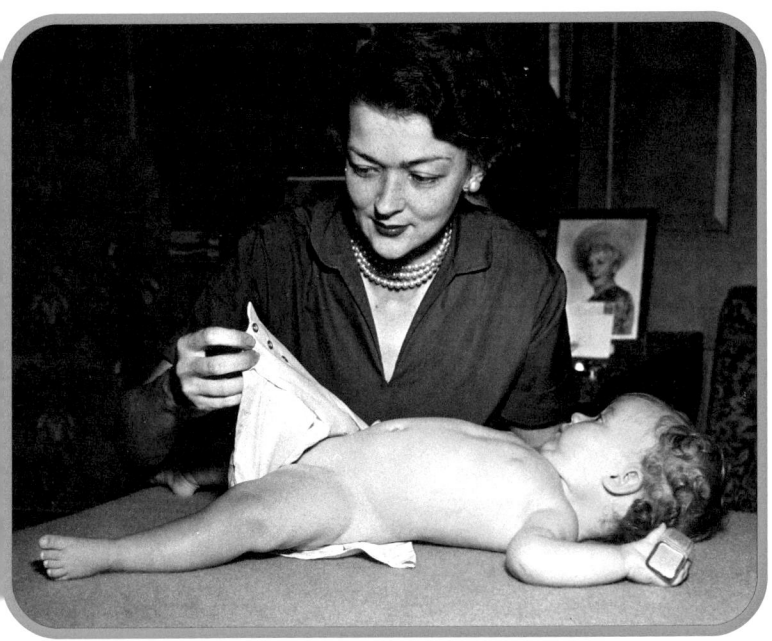

*Marion Donovan's disposable diaper cover was made of nylon parachute cloth and featured metal and plastic snaps. It launched at Saks Fifth Avenue in 1949 and was immediately successful.*

## The Problem Without a Name

Having a home and family brought satisfaction to many women. But they weren't all as content as those smiling women in the television shows. TV personality Garry Moore was right. Many housewives in the 1950s were lonely and bored. Watching television and shopping, however, didn't always help. Throughout the 1950s, a large number of women visited their doctors, complaining of aches and tiredness. Mostly, they blamed themselves for their uneasy and anxious feelings. "There must be some-thing wrong with me," they'd tell their doctors. More often than not, the doctors agreed and prescribed iron pills to give them more energy or mild tranquilizers to ease their discontent. Something else was happening too. More and more couples were divorcing. But there weren't any television programs about that social phenomenon. TV families such as *Bachelor Father* and *My Three Sons* told stories about men raising children on their own. Death, not divorce, had left them as single parents.

In 1960 the media began to write about the discontent many house-wives experienced. "Why Young Mothers Feel Trapped" was the title of an article in *Redbook* magazine. *Good Housekeeping, Newsweek*, and a CBS television documentary were among the popular media that also explored the issue. Women felt like "shut-ins" in their own homes, "left out" of the mainstream of life, reported the *New York Times* on June 28, 1960.

By this time, Betty Friedan had been interviewing women of her own genera-tion for ten years. Like her, most had grad-uated from college, married, and moved to the suburbs to raise their children. Many carpooled with other moms, shut-tling their kids to and from Little League baseball games and Girl Scout meetings. In her interviews, Friedan discovered something else she and most of these women shared. "When we were growing up, many of us could not see ourselves beyond the age of twenty-one," she wrote. "We had no image of our own future, of ourselves as women." A woman, not yet

*Betty Friedan signs copies of* The Feminine Mystique *twelve years after its 1963 publication. The best-selling book created tremendous controversy. It also sparked a new wave of feminism and eventually became a classic in the field of feminist literature.*

forty years old, told Friedan, "Nobody ever looked us in the eye and said you have to decide what you want to do with your life, besides being your husband's wife and children's mother." Friedan called the discontent so many American women felt "the problem without a name." And then she gave it one: the feminine mystique.

*Mystique* means "mystery" or "secrecy." Friedan said she chose this phrase because most women couldn't pinpoint a specific reason for feeling discontented. Some felt angry for no apparent reason. Others felt like crying, but they didn't understand what was making them so

> # "Nobody ever looked us in the eye and said you have to decide what you want to do with your life, besides being your husband's wife and children's mother."

— Betty Friedan, 1963

sad. These were not the troubled housewives struggling to make ends meet who had appeared on the television show *Queen for a Day*. These women had secure incomes, homes, and families. Even those who worked outside the home—and a great many did—felt guilty about leaving their children. Most women blamed themselves for these feelings. Something had to be wrong with them if they weren't as happy as the women they saw in magazines or on television.

Published in 1963, Friedan's book *The Feminine Mystique* became a best seller. Thousands of women readers discovered within its pages that others shared the same frustrations they experienced. Many began to realize that they weren't freaks after all. Other women felt just as they did! Hundreds of readers wrote to Friedan after reading her book. They shared with her their own disenchantments. The book created social controversy. Friedan had pointed a finger of blame at the U.S. educational system, which encouraged women to study "feminine" subjects such as family life and household management rather than science, mathematics, and business management. She also blamed popular media, including women's magazines and television programs that portrayed unrealistic images of happy housewives. Friedan quoted a magazine editor who told her, "Our readers are housewives, full time. . . . They are not interested in national or international affairs. They are only interested in the family and the home."

These assumptions about American women were false, wrote Friedan. But the assumptions explained why women's magazines featured stories on baby care and recipes rather than social and political issues such as civil rights and nuclear testing.

Not everyone agreed with Friedan. A book reviewer for the *New York Times* said the book was full of sweeping generalities and exaggerations. Even if Friedan's statements were true, the book reviewer argued, "What is to stop a woman who is interested in national and international affairs from reading magazines that deal with those subjects?"

# The Pill Puts Parenthood on Hold

For years, the makers of Lady Clairol hair coloring had used sex appeal to sell their products to women. Magazine advertisements asked, "Is it true . . . *blondes* have more fun?" Yes! said the makers of Miss Clairol. Men adored blondes, advertisements claimed. A woman with "mousey brown" hair could change her appearance at home in less than an hour by using Miss Clairol products.

Advertising copywriter Shirley Polykoff created the Miss Clairol slogan "Do blondes have more fun?" In the 1960s, she came up with a second catchy slogan: "Does she or doesn't she?" Miss Clairol claimed that their product was so natural looking that no one could tell whether a woman dyed her hair or not. The phrase, however, was ambiguous, suggesting a sexual meaning. Does she or doesn't she . . . go all the way? (Or in more blunt terms—have sexual relationships with men.)

*The images in this ad show that having more fun involves the presence of a man. The Clairol ads, with their sexual overtones, are said to have caused the number of women wishing to be blondes to jump nearly 500 percent.*

In 1960 the development of the birth control pill gave women a legal means of preventing pregnancy. As a result, sexual promiscuity was increasingly discussed and even promoted in popular culture. Novels such as *Sex and the Single Girl* hit the best-seller list. Films such as *Splendor in the Grass* explored teenage sexuality. Even before the pill hit the market, newspaper headlines announced a rise in teenage pregnancy. In an article titled "Illegitimacy Rise Alarm Agencies," published on August 9, 1959, the *New York Times* reported that five thousand babies each year were born to girls under the age of fifteen. Educational groups and alarmed parents called for sex education programs in school so that young women could be better informed about the biology of their bodies. Meanwhile, popular culture continued to explore women's sexual freedom and advertisements continued to use sex appeal as a persuasive selling strategy.

What Friedan had termed the "problem with no name" was not the fault of the media, argued the reviewer, but of the women themselves. The reviewer, incidentally, was a woman, Lucy Freeman.

## Whether women agreed or disagreed with *The Feminine Mystique*, the book shattered the image of the happy housewife.

Another reviewer said Friedan was way off base. She was writing about neurotic, or mentally disturbed, housewives and not the majority of women, some reviewers suggested. The book triggered hostility from the author's suburban neighbors, as well. They stopped inviting her to luncheons and dinner parties. Her children also lost friendships. "I practically had to flee my own crabgrass-overgrown yard to keep from being burned at the stake," said Friedan. Eventually, she and her family sold their house and moved to New York City.

Whether women agreed or disagreed with *The Feminine Mystique*, the book shattered the image of the happy housewife and consumer so common in magazine advertisements and television programming. As a result of Friedan's book, women started talking to one another about education and work opportunities. They discussed, too, a desire for equal wages. Why was it, they asked, that a woman received less money than a man for doing the same job? They talked about the way the popular media portrayed women. Many women found the courage to take charge of a new part of their lives. They did not turn their backs on their husbands or children. They were still wives and mothers. But many discovered that it was OK to be an individual with interests and desires of her own.

Women often stood in lines in bookstores to get Betty Friedan's autograph on their copies of *The Feminine Mystique*. Many told her the same thing: your book changed my life. In addition to signing her name, Friedan would write an inscription in the book: "Courage to us all on the new road."

# Chapter Three
# Teen Scenes

Legs and feet of five teenage girls wearing dog collar anklets on their socks, 1953

We listened to this music in the darkness of our bedrooms, driving around in our parents' cars, on the beach, making out with some boy, and we danced to it—usually with other girls—in the soda shops, basements, and gymnasiums of America. . . . In this music, we found solidarity as girls.

—Susan Douglas, *Where the Girls Are: Growing Up Female with the Mass Media*

# One of the most popular children's shows

of the 1950s was the *Mickey Mouse Club*. Created by cartoonist Walt Disney, the show began the same year that Disney opened his amusement park in Southern California: Disneyland. The *Mickey Mouse Club* featured a troupe of twenty-four children called Mouseketeers. They were ordinary kids, not professional actors. Walt Disney wanted his Mouseketeers to be positive role models for American children. The Mouseketeers wore T-shirts with their names in block letters across the front. They also wore beanie caps with mouse ears. They sang songs. They introduced cartoons with a magical chant that children across the United States soon began to imitate: Meeska Mooseka Mouseketeer, Mouse Kartoon Time Now Is Here. Soon, kids across the United States were also wearing those funny mouse ears and picking their favorite Mouseketeers. More often than not, the favorite was Annette.

Annette Funicello was twelve years old when Walt Disney saw her in a school dance recital in Burbank, California. He sensed at once that the shy, curly-haired brunette had star potential, and he hired her. Annette (she was so well known that the media usually referred to her by only her first name) received bags of fan mail each month. As many as six thousand letters came from girls who thought of her as a best friend and boys who often asked her to go steady.

After three years, the *Mickey Mouse Club* went off the air. Annette had matured into an attractive, though still shy, teenager. Disney featured her in other TV shows, including *Zorro*, and in movies. By the 1960s, she had hit songs on the radio and hit movies in theaters. She also appeared on countless covers of teen magazines. The

The Mickey Mouse Club *was made up of the talented and endearing group of mouse-eared young stars known as the Mouseketeers. Most popular among them was Annette Funicello (shown here in 1956, far left in front row),* who went on to a film and music career.

Mouseketeer had become an all-American teen idol, the sweet girl-next-door whom every boy wished he could take to the prom.

Some baby boomers were no longer babies. Nor were they Mouseketeers, either. They were teenagers. There have always been teenagers. But these teenagers had more than just their ages in common. According to the media, they shared common characteristics, behaviors, and interests. They dressed alike, wearing bobby socks and blue jeans. In the 1960s, boys grew their hair long and girls wore miniskirts. Teens ate the same kinds of foods—sodas and malted milk shakes, hamburgers, french fries, and pizza. They spoke slang: *To dig* someone or something meant "to like him, her, or it." To be *square* meant "to be unpopular and old-fashioned." Many teenagers liked the same kinds of entertainment—horror and science-fiction films shown in drive-in movie theaters and rock-and-roll music. Some media images suggested teenagers were reckless delinquents who vandalized communities and fought in street gangs.

Generalizing about teenagers, however, was impossible in the 1950s and 1960s (and still is). "I wear blue jeans and dig rock 'n' roll. I am not a delinquent," wrote one teenager to *Time* magazine in 1956. But *Time* also published a second letter in the same issue from a boy who proclaimed his dislike of rock and roll. "I am 14 years old and am no square and I hate every note of it."

By 1963 a whole new genre of entertainment had been born: the teen movie. Annette Funicello is shown standing next to a promotional billboard for her latest film release, Beach Party.

Despite the contradictions, one thing was true for many American teenagers, especially white teenagers, during these decades: they had more money to spend than their parents had had. And how they spent it influenced popular media. Teenage girls, in particular, would influence popular music in significant ways, from surfing songs to rock and roll and hard rock.

## "It's Neat to Spend!"

In 1956 studies estimated that 13 million American teenagers had an average income of about $10.55 a week. They earned the money from working after school or weekends, or they received it as allowances for doing chores around the house. Teenagers say, "It's neat to spend," reported *Newsweek* magazine.

So what were American female teenagers buying? First on the list were records. Girls in suburban communities spent hours in their bedrooms or in the recreation rooms of their parents' homes playing 45s on their record players. A 45 was a vinyl disc holding recordings of two songs, one on each side. The sale of these single hits soared. So did the sale of teen fan magazines. Stories about male stars, such as Fabian, Troy Donahue, or Ricky Nelson, told readers about the kind of girls they liked.

Teenage girls often communicated by telephone. Popular teen magazines, such as *Seventeen* and *American Girl*, published advertisements for a new type of bedside telephone called the Princess. Ads showed

*From the mid-1950s through the 1960s, the average home record player could be set for three different speeds—78 , 45, and 33⅓ revolutions per minute (rpm). Teen fans of rock and roll preferred the 45 disc. It was smaller than the other two (7 inches [18 cm] vs. 12 inches [30 cm]) and had a large hole in the center that required an insert to make it fit on the small spindle of a record player.*

that a typical American teenage girl (viewed at this time as being white and middle class) could curl up on her bed in a nest of stuffed animals and chat away for hours on her very own phone. "It's little. It's lovely. It lights!" was the advertising motto. It came in powder blue and pink. In the center of the dial was an etching of a Cinderella-like crown and the words *The Princess*.

On a Friday night, a teenage girl might go to a dance at the local YWCA (Young Women's Christian Association). If she were old enough to drive, she and her girlfriends might pile into a car, contributing a dime or a quarter each toward a tank of gasoline, and drive to the local drive-in restaurant. In some drive-ins, female carhops dressed like majorettes on roller skates. They rolled through the parking lot to take orders, then returned minutes later with a tray of hamburgers, french fries, and milk shakes. The tray hooked right on the car window.

Dating cost money, but boys usually paid for dates in this era. A popular date was the drive-in movie. In 1958 more than eight thousand drive-in theaters across the country entertained families, who could go to the movies without having to pay a babysitter. When the sun set, the giant, outdoor movie screens came to life. Some people, however, called these drive-ins passion pits. In the dark privacy of parked cars, teenagers "made out."

A carhop writes down a food order for a couple at a drive-in restaurant. The food will be served on a tray that attaches to the car at window level. The scene is from 1954, the height of drive-in popularity.

They kissed, touched, and sometimes went further. Some concerned parents thought drive-in theaters encouraged sexual temptations. But many teenagers saw drive-ins as a place to hang out with their friends and not just their boyfriends. Drive-ins were so popular with

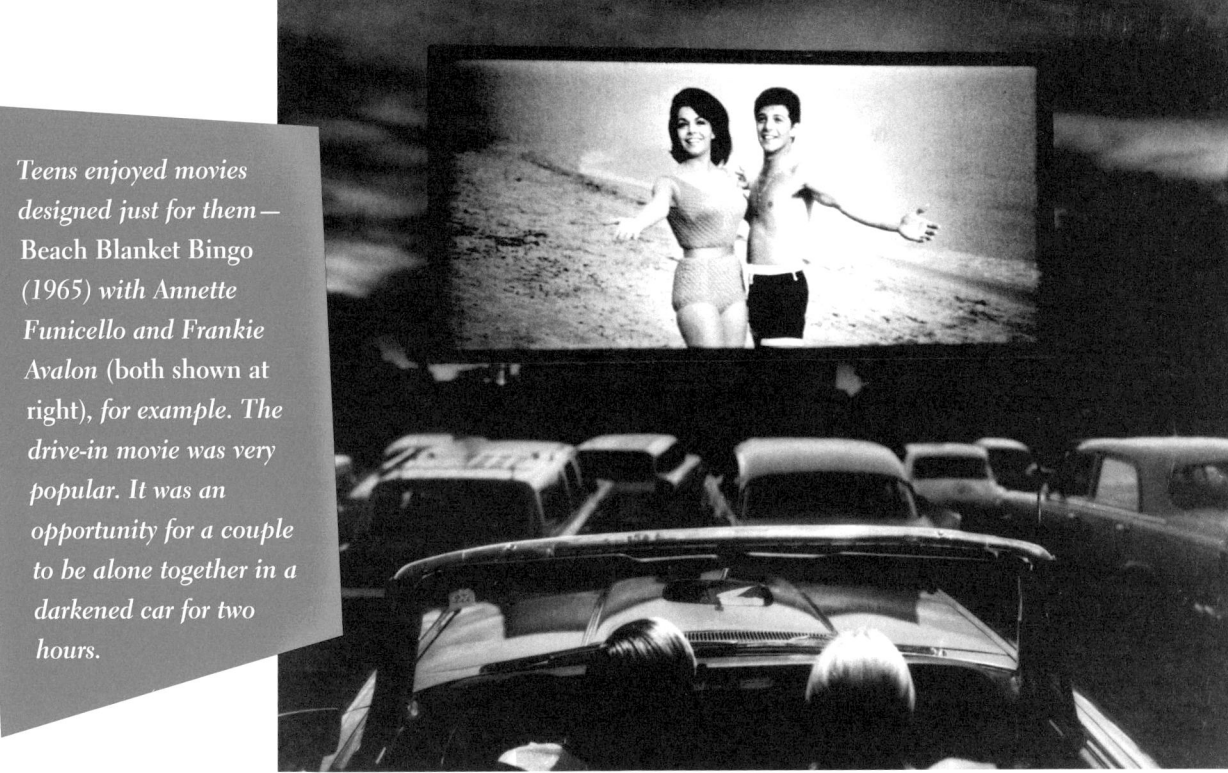

*Teens enjoyed movies designed just for them— Beach Blanket Bingo (1965) with Annette Funicello and Frankie Avalon (both shown at right), for example. The drive-in movie was very popular. It was an opportunity for a couple to be alone together in a darkened car for two hours.*

teenagers that Hollywood produced B movies just for these theaters. B movies were often low-budget science-fiction and horror films starring teenage characters.

Comic books, shampoos, facial creams, pimple medications, perfumes, and bathing suits—the teenage shopping list grew longer and longer as more businesses paid attention to the likes and dislikes of teenagers.

## The Gidget Phenomenon

During the summer of 1956, fifteen-year-old Kathy Kohner hung out on a beach in Malibu, California. She strayed away from the other girls, who were sunbathing, to watch a group of older guys surfing. They kicked sand in her face when she pestered them for surfing lessons. "Don't you know girls can't surf?" they told her. Day after day, she returned. Trying to impress the surfers, she made peanut-butter-and-jelly sandwiches at home and passed them out to the guys on the beach. "Am I bothering you?" she once asked Scooter, a surfer.

"You're breathing, aren't you?" he answered.

"I'm going to be here whether you like it or not," she said. Eventually, she got a surfboard of her own, and the lessons began. Still, the guys played practical jokes on her, such as burying her surfboard in the sand. Not only was she a girl, she was tiny—not quite 5 feet (152 cm) tall and weighing maybe 100 pounds (45 kg), soaking wet with salt water. And she was as young as the surfers' kid sisters. Most of the surfers were nineteen years old and older. They gave her a nickname, a combination of *girl* and *midget*: Gidget.

# Good Girl versus the Hook

The story first appeared in a Dear Abby newspaper advice column on November 8, 1960. A frightened teenage girl had written to Abby:

If you are interested in teenagers, you will print this story. I don't know whether it's true or not, but it doesn't matter because it served its purpose on me.

A fellow and his date pulled into their favorite 'lovers' lane' to listen to the radio and do a little necking. The music was interrupted by an announcer who said there was an escaped convict in the area who had served time for rape and robbery. He was described as having a hook instead of a right hand. The couple became frightened and drove away. When the boy took his girl home, he went around to open the car door for her. Then he saw—a hook on the door handle! I don't think I will ever park to make out as long as I live. I hope this does the same for other kids.

The girl who wrote to Abby said the story had "served its purpose on me." What was that purpose? Perhaps the story was a warning that a good girl would never have gone parking with a boy in the first place. Naughty girls who did could lose their lives! But was the lovers' lane story true?

Abby was Abigail Van Buren, and her advice column appeared in the *Chicago Tribune* every day throughout most of the 1950s and all of the 1960s. (Her column would eventually be internationally syndicated and, written by her daughter, still be popular in the twenty-first century.) As for the hook, the letter the teenager sent to the newspaper was probably real, but the story was not. It was an urban legend, or a story repeated so often that people think it must be true. Urban legends usually involve danger or a strange coincidence that reflects some fear society has. The story is meant to teach an important lesson. Perhaps that is why Abby printed it in her advice column. "The Hook" was one of the best-known urban legends among teenagers in the 1950s and early 1960s.

*Author and Dear Abby columnist Abigail Van Buren sits at her typewriter in 1958. Her identical twin sister, Ann Landers, was also an advice columnist.*

"I'm not a gidget," she snapped back. "My name is Kathryn!"

Her spunk eventually won them over. That summer Kathy kept a journal. On July 22, she wrote: "I went to the beach again today. . . . I just love it down there. . . . I went out surfing about three times but only caught one wave."

That summer Kathy's father began hearing her tales of strange surfing creatures called Tubesteak and Moondoggie. Kathy admitted she had a crush on some of the guys, but she was no "beach bunny." That's what the guys called the girls who watched them surf. Kathy's real love was for the sport itself. Her father listened as she described waves as "bitchin'." It means "really strong and powerful waves." He picked up other surfing slang as well: *shooting the curl* means "riding in and out of the hollow part of a wave as it crested over." *Hanging ten* means "standing with the toes over the nose of the surfboard," *Wiping out* means "falling off."

Kathy wasn't the only surfer girl at Malibu Point, but she was the only Gidget. Her father asked if he might write a book about her experiences. She agreed. A year later, his paperback novel titled *Gidget, the Little Girl with Big Ideas* hit the bookstores. It turned out to be a best seller.

In 1959 the movie *Gidget*, based on the book, was a sellout in movie theaters across the United States. Suddenly surfer girls were everywhere!

*Sixteen-year-old surfer Kathy Kohner (nicknamed Gidget) stands on a Malibu, California, beach in 1957. Kohner's father turned her tales of beach culture and surfing into a series of novels.*

In surfing slang, *cowabunga* means "wild joy while catching a big wave." Gidget was a cowabunga commercial success. Both the book and the movie created a media sensation. Movies, popular music, and even advertisers hopped on Gidget's wild wave. The original Gidget (the character in the Kohner book) was a rebel. She cursed, she smoked, and she hung out with the guys. Hollywood altered the image, however, making Gidget more perky than potty-mouthed. They also changed her physically. She was still gidget—small, but she was no longer brunette. She was blonde.

Gidget gave rise to a series of what came to be known as beach blanket movies. *Beach Party*, *Bikini Beach*, and *Beach Blanket Bingo* starred former Mouseketeer Annette Funicello. Annette did not curse or smoke as the book's Gidget did. Walt Disney, who produced the movies, protected Annette's sweetheart image by insisting that her two-piece bathing suit did not reveal her navel. Still, Annette hung out on the beach with the boys, and they still wanted her to be their girl.

> "I went to the beach again today. . . . I just love it down there. . . . I went out surfing about three times but only caught one wave."
>
> —Kathy Kohner, 1956

Surfing music became popular on the radio. This was a new type of rock music, featuring mostly guitars. Jan and Dean sang about a California town called Surf City. The Beach Boys sang that everyone—well, as least everyone who was young— was surfing. The beach was the place to go, not just for the surfing, but also to be together. The musicians in these all-male rock groups were young, white, usually suntanned, and blond. They seemed to like their girls suntanned and blonde too.

How did this music affect the nation's females who didn't live on the West Coast? Luckily, other musicians and songs became big hits during the 1950s and 1960s. Landlocked girls couldn't surf,

*During the 1950s, children as young as ten began to have their own money to buy transistor radios and 45s recordings. Rock legend Elvis Presley (above) is who they chose to listen to.*

but they still had musical idols to imitate and adore.

## The Teenyboppers

The media called them teenyboppers. They were teenage girls, and they made rock-and-roll musicians big, big stars. They bought their records. They bought fan magazines that published photographs of the musicians. They bought tickets for their concerts. Sometimes, to the amazement of the media and the shock of their parents, they became a frenzied mob and mauled their idols. Teenyboppers were a new media phenomenon. Through the music of performers such as Elvis Presley, Diana Ross and the Supremes, and the Beatles, girls would begin defining who they were and what they valued.

On December 15, 1956, thousands of teenyboppers packed the Youth Building at the Louisiana State Fairgrounds in Shreveport. Their idol Elvis Presley would perform during a live television broadcast of *The Louisiana Hayride*. The building could hold an audience of ten thousand. Anticipating a packed house and a good deal of teenybopper madness, the management built a fence in front of the stage and set the chairs 30 feet (9 meters) back from the fence. When the doors opened, the teenyboppers rushed in like a flash flood, pushing chairs as close to the fence as possible. The police could not stop them.

Elvis was known to travel in a pink Cadillac. The management dressed another man who resembled Elvis in stage clothes and drove him in the pink car to the front of the building. The female fans mobbed the decoy in the car while the real Elvis slipped in the back door and got ready to perform. The screaming began when he came onstage. The fans screamed during every song. They never stopped screaming.

Frank Page witnessed the spectacle and was terrified. "I had never heard ten thousand teenagers screaming at the top of their lungs before," he would later write. "I had the feeling that something had to happen, either panic or a riot or even that the very walls would crumble."

Even after Elvis left the stage at the end of the performance, the teenyboppers screamed. The announcer tried to calm the audience. "Please young people . . . Elvis has left the building. He has gotten in his car and driven away."

His appeal wasn't just his music. It was also his sneering lip and his gyrating, swivel-hipped movements. The teenyboppers loved it. "He's a hunk, a hunk of burning love!" said Kay Wheeler, the teenybopper who formed the first Elvis Presley fan club. Parents, however, were not happy. Most thought that Elvis was

*By the mid-1960s, the Beatles had taken over Elvis in the hearts of teenage girls. This audience listens in tears of ecstasy to a 1967 Beatles concert in New York. It was a common reaction to the singers' British-style charm.*

vulgar and a bad influence on their daughters—and sons too.

The media called Elvis the King of Rock and Roll. But it was the teenyboppers who gave the king his crown.

A few years later, another group of rock idols captured the teenyboppers' hearts. They were four young men from Liverpool, England, and they looked nothing like Elvis. They wore suits and skinny ties and had long, shaggy hair, which they shook as they sang. The moment the Beatles stepped onto the stage in Memphis, Tennessee, the audience of mostly young women went berserk. "Emily Strider," reported the *Memphis Commercial Appeal*, "started to cry. Then she started to scream. Then she started shaking her head wildly and pounding her knees with her fists."

Fans held Elvis Is Dead signs at some Beatles concert, suggesting that the king had lost his kingdom. But that wasn't quite true. Elvis was still rockin' and rollin'. But a new generation of teenyboppers had fallen in love with Paul, John, George, and Ringo. The media gave these fans a different label, Beatlemaniacs, even though their behavior was much the same. At the Memphis concert, more than seven thou-

sand Beatlemaniacs cried and shrieked so loudly that few could hear the music. Across the country, wherever the rock group performed, newspapers and magazines printed photographs of teenage girls with mouths open wide in mid-scream and cheeks wet with tears.

The Beatles looked and sounded different from American rock stars. What frightened parents, however, was not the boys' "mop tops" or the lyrics they sang about wanting to hold hands. Those sounded innocent enough. What was disturbing was the way the girls reacted. They fell madly in love, emphasis on *madly*. At concerts some wore signs around their necks saying, "I love Paul." The girl fanatics threw jelly beans and stuffed animals onstage. A few even tossed underwear.

Chris Sum was twelve years old when she saw the Beatles in concert in Chicago. "My legs turned to jelly, my mouth hung

> *"My legs turned to jelly, my mouth hung open, all I could do was stare."* —Chris Sum, 2004, speaking of the Beatles in 1964

# The Juvenile Delinquent Scare

In the 1950s, newspaper headlines began focusing on a different breed of teenager—the juvenile delinquent, or JD. These were the tough guys and girls. They wore leather jackets and tight jeans. They drag raced on public highways in stolen cars. They vandalized property, drank beer, and mocked adults just for the fun of it. The worst of them carried knives and, if challenged, used them on one another.

The typical JD was male. But females, too, made headlines. Their crimes were not as violent but were just as disturbing, because the criminals were girls. They ran away from home. They shoplifted. They hung out with the bad boys.

Some experts blamed the growing rate of teenage crime on television. A study of television programs taken during the week of January 4 to 10, 1953, showed that in that week alone, 3,421 acts or threats of violence were broadcast. These weren't actual crimes but fictional dramas. Still, experts worried that exposure to violence on television, day after day, week after week, was harmful to youth.

Others blamed rock-and-roll music. Some religious leaders wanted the music banned from the radio, reported *Time* magazine. Rock and roll was seen as the music of hoodlums and roughnecks. Teenagers wrote letters of protest to the magazine. They called adults fuddy-duddies and hypocrites who had forgotten what it was like to be young and to have fun.

*Female teens were no longer just the girlfriends of male gang members. They formed their own gangs in inner cities and rode in their own motorcycle packs in the suburbs.*

open, all I could do was stare," she said. Her parents might not have approved, but there was "no way" they could stop her. Beatlemania swept the country, and all parents could do was hope, in time, the sickness would pass.

Were these fanatic fans always females? Media images suggested so. Boys also listened to, purchased, and even imitated the Beatles' music. Many grew their hair long, adopting the group's mop-top-style. Young male fans, however, didn't cry and throw candy during concerts. If they did, the magazines didn't print pictures of their screaming, tear-wet faces.

## The Girl Group Sound

Whenever people asked Marcie Blane what she wanted to be, she answered that she wanted to be Bobby's girl, as in his steady date. Nothing was more important in her life that to have Bobby as a boyfriend. Marcie Blane was a songwriter and singer in the 1960s, and "Bobby's Girl" was the big hit single that made sixteen-year-old Blane an overnight success.

A nifty little invention called the transistor made it possible for teenagers to carry lightweight, pocket-sized radios with them anywhere they went. "Bobby's Girl" could be heard on the beach, on the playground, in the backyard, and on the street corner—anywhere teenagers hung out. The transistor radio was a teenager's delight. Unlike the family TV, sitting big and heavy in the living room, the transistor gave teens freedom of choice. They could choose their favorite AM radio station and the type of music they preferred.

Pop music was softer than rock and roll, with a greater emphasis on harmony. Rock lyrics full of nonsense syllables in hits such as "Tuttie Frutti" could sometimes be puzzling. Pop music had its share of nonsense phrases too, such as "nibby, knobby, nooby" in the song "Good Morning Starshine." More often, though, pop songs told stories about teenage love. Shelley Fabares sang about "Johnny Angel," a guy who has something that she just couldn't resist. But oh! she lamented, he doesn't seem to even know she exists. Shelley turns down other guys who ask her out so that she can be right next to the telephone in case Johnny calls. But if he doesn't know she exists, how can he call her? Logic wasn't an essential ingredient in mixing up a pop music hit.

Both male and female singers created pop music hits. Brian Hyland's hit single was about a girl who wears a very tiny yellow polka-dot bikini. But she is so embarrassed by how revealing it is that she stays in the water, afraid to come out. Girl groups were

*The girl groups were known for their careful harmonies and high-end production. Their lyrics spoke directly to teenage emotions. At far left are the Shirelles, who established the girl group sound in 1960. They were followed quickly by (from left) the Dixie Cups, the Ronettes, and the one group that was able to compete with rock music in the late 1960s—the Supremes.*

particularly successful in the late 1950s and early 1960s. The Shirelles, the Dixie Cups, Diana Ross and the Supremes, the Ronettes—the names of the groups differed, but the singers were all teenage girls who longed for love. They didn't play instruments, but they performed their song-stories like actresses, and the fan magazines loved them! Page after page discussed their hairdos, dresses, and love lives. Many of these new teenage pop stars were women of color. The Supremes, for example, captured the covers of teen magazines—the first time that young women of color got prominent media attention.

Social historian Susan Douglas grew up listening to girl group music. The song-stories were something she could act out, as well.

And depending on the lyrics, she could assume any number of different personalities. When singing "He's a Rebel," she could pretend to be a faithful girlfriend defiantly standing by the boy she loved. Other songs offered other roles to play. Douglas explained, "As girls listened to their radios and record players, they could be martyrs to love . . . fearsome Amazons protecting their men, devoted selfless girlfriends, [or] taunting, competitive brats."

Carole King and Ellie Greenwich wrote many of the hit songs the girl groups sang. They weren't the only women in the business, but they were the only two women behind the scenes who did it all— wrote lyrics and music, sang, and produced. Production involved working with the bands and managing the technical elements of recording the song. "I never felt that being a woman was an obstacle or an advantage," said Carole King. "Nobody has ever said, 'You can't do this, you're a woman.'"

"Da Doo Ron Ron" was Ellie Greenwich's first big hit. It was about first love at first sight. The song, which kept repeating the title syllables, wasn't meant to be meaningful. It was just a happy sound that kept the beat. "In the '60s people wanted to be happy," said Greenwich. She wrote songs that anybody could sing. And everybody did. Whether performed by the Shangri-Las, the Crystals, or the Dixie Cups—Greenwich's songs often went gold (meaning they sold five hundred thousand copies) or platinum (one million).

Some songs weren't altogether happy, however. The lyrics suggested that girls often took risks. They could be attracted to a boy who was a rebel or an outsider. In one song, a girl falls in love with "The Leader of the Pack." The "pack" was a motorcycle gang, and in the final verse, the leader crashes and dies, but the Shangri-Las vowed to love him always.

The spotlight was bright for a girl group with a hit single. Often the light faded quickly as the next hit single by the next group soared to the top. Most groups lasted just a few years. Then the spotlight would dim, and the group's name would slip into pop music history.

> *"I never felt that being a woman was an obstacle or an advantage. Nobody has ever said, 'You can't do this, you're a woman.'"*
>
> —Carole King, 1989

# "You Don't Own Me"

Leslie Gore was just fifteen when she sang her way to the top of the pop music charts. "It's My Party" tells the story of a birthday turned bad. The birthday girl's date is Johnny, but he sneaks out with Judy. When the couple returns, Judy is wearing Johnny's ring, and the birthday girl begins to bawl.

Teenage boys listening to songs like these might have gotten the impression that a girl's sole ambition in life was to have a steady boyfriend. They might have also thought that girls were submissive. In April 1963, Peggy March had a hit single, "I Will Follow Him," in which she vowed she'd follow her boyfriend anywhere he went or no matter what he did because she loved him.

At sixteen Leslie Gore was tired of what she called "wimpy" love songs. With the help of composer Quincy Jones, she recorded a pop single with a very different message. The girl in the song was downright bossy. She scolded boys who tried to control her or change the way she looked. Clearly, this time Gore wasn't going to cry over a cheating boyfriend.

*At the age of eighteen, Lesley Gore gave up her highly successful singing career to enter college.*

"You Don't Own Me" was an even bigger hit than "It's My Party," climbing all the way to number two on the record charts. The song gave Gore much more than fame and fortune, however. It gave her strength. "Imagine being 16 and being able to shake a finger and say, 'Don't tell me what to do,'" she said. "Even though I was just acting and playing (grown-up), it still felt very powerful." The lyrics were so powerful, in fact, that Gore decided that her record company didn't own her, either. She understood the pop music business could be fickle and that the next girl group with a hit song could knock her off the charts for good. "I had a good brain in my head," she said. And so at eighteen, the teen idol enrolled in Sarah Lawrence College in New York to major in English. Going to college would ruin her career, her agent argued. Gore didn't care. Off to college she went. And college did interfere with her career. Her last hit single was "California Nights" in 1967. In later years, however, she performed in concerts and composed songs for movie sound tracks.

Berry Gordy was the founder of Motown Records. *Motown* was short for "Motortown," another name for Detroit, Michigan. In the 1950s, Detroit was home to the booming automobile manufacturing industry. It was also home to many African Americans. Gordy's Motown Records featured the talent of young black musicians, both male and female. Their success was part sound and part showmanship. Gordy hired Maxine Powell, a black woman who owned a modeling school in Chicago, to teach his girls—and guys too—poise and confidence. The Temptations, the Supremes, Martha Reeves and the Vandellas, and the Four Tops—they all had tremendous talent. They could sing, and they could dance. But they lacked style and sophistication at first.

"Some of them were rude, crude, uncouth and straight from the streets of Detroit," Maxine Powell said. For two hours a day, they studied with Professor Powell (a nickname they gave her). She taught them how to speak, correcting bad grammar. She taught them how to walk, with shoulders back and head lifted. She taught them refinement. At first, they resisted her. But she convinced them that she was there to uplift their lives: "I told them they had to be prepared to perform before kings and queens." In this way, Powell created a media image. The Motown groups were more than teen idols or pop culture icons. They were role models for young people. Whites as well as minorities respected them. By shaping their media images, Powell and Gordy gave their young performers pride as well as profitable careers in show business.

"Before meeting her," black singer Martha Reeves said of Powell, "I never felt I had a place in society, but she taught us that all doors would eventually open, and she was absolutely right."

## The Queen of Mod

A teenager wrote to the editor of *Time* magazine, thanking him for running an article on Twiggy. If there is hope for her, the teen wrote, then there's hope for me.

Twiggy was Leslie Hornby, a seventeen-year-old fashion model from Great Britain. At 5 feet 6 inches (168 cm) tall and weighing about 90 pounds (41 kg), she was skinny and flat chested. Her legs were like twigs, her friends had teased her, which is how she got her professional modeling name. American fashion magazines in the mid-1960s were all about the Twiggy look: miniskirts that revealed a good deal of thigh, a boyishly short haircut, and large, heavily lined eyes with extra long, thick lashes.

# From Neat to Groovy

Teenage girls of the late 1960s looked quite a bit different from teenagers just a decade earlier. In the 1950s and early 1960s, a girl might wear a pleated or a full circle skirt with a sweater set to school. (A sweater set was a matching pair of sweaters, one pullover with short sleeves and one with buttons, worn one over the other.) To give her skirt fullness, she wore a net or nylon petticoat. A colorful scarf, perhaps held down by a set of scatter pins, was a "neat" (or cool) fashion accessory.

In the early 1960s, skirts and sweaters were still the fashion trend for school days, but the skirts were A-lined rather than pleated or full circles. And they were shorter too—but not too short. One way a teacher or a principal might determine if a girl's skirt was the right length was to have her kneel. If the hem didn't touch the floor, the skirt was too short.

As the decade progressed, the popularity of British cultural icons, including the Beatles and Twiggy, changed fashion again. Skirts rose higher. Jackets were fringed. Bell-bottom blue jeans hugged the hips. Boots and platform shoes were in, and the higher the heel the better. Bold patterns and colors were "groovy."

Although the styles changed over the two decades, from circle skirts to miniskirts, from neck scarves to love beads, one thing didn't change. Teenagers adopted fashion styles as a way of expressing themselves—who they were or wanted to become.

*The dress code for teens of the 1950s was to strictly conform to the fashion of the times, thus making their clothes very similar to each other's as shown by the young women at top. The fashion of the 1960s was another matter entirely. Nonconformity was a style in itself, leading to diverse fashion statements such as the two outfits at right.*

*Leslie Hornsby, known as Twiggy, is shown here in 1966 as she poses in a transparent plastic dress. Weighing in at just over 90 pounds (40 kg), she looked nothing like the curvaceous long-haired models of the early 1960s. The* New York Times *summed up her look by describing her as the eleven-year-old boy next door.*

"Her face must be her fortune," *Time* wrote about Twiggy, "because her body certainly is not."

American teenage girls (and a great number of older women too) went *mod*—shorthand for "modern," or the Twiggy look. Gone were the restrictive girdles, nylon stockings, and garters of the 1950s. Short skirts required a new invention—panty hose. Girls stepped into them and tugged them up to their waists. Gone, too, were stiff, unnaturally pointy bras so popular during the perky sweater-girl years of the 1950s. Some women opted not to wear a bra at all. Achieving the slim-hipped Twiggy look, however, required more than just removing restrictive clothing. The number of teenage girls dieting increased significantly.

When an interviewer asked Twiggy if she thought she was beautiful, Twiggy answered no. In fact, she admitted that she didn't have much of a figure and that her willowy body bothered her. She ate all the time, *Time* reported, especially banana ice cream and hot fudge.

The mod look of the 1960s included fishnet stockings, go-go boots (short, usually white), and wildly patterned and brightly colored fabrics—hot orange, lime green, or shocking pink.

Twiggy earned as much as twenty-five hundred dollars a week, the *New York Times* reported. But by 1970, at the age of twenty, she was retiring from the fashion business. By then miniskirts had become maxis with hemlines down to the ankles. Maxis would soon give way to pantsuits. And mod was yesterday's news.

# The Flower Child Generation

In 1967 Scott McKenzie had a hit single titled "San Francisco." According to the lyrics, young people were gathering in this northern California city for a summer of love. And they were wearing flowers in their hair.

The were ages fifteen through twenty-five. During that summer of 1967, more than one hundred thousand young people traveled across country to San Francisco. They gathered in groups on street corners—the most popular was the intersection of Haight and Ashbury streets. Summer was typically a time of vacation and freedom from schools and other restrictions. These teenagers and young adults, however, were celebrating a different kind of freedom. They believed a new age of peace and love was possible and that their generation could change the world.

*Hip* was a slang term of the times meaning "popular or cool." The media called the young people "hippies" or "flower children" because of their appearance. Both men and women wore headbands or flowers in their shoulder-length hair. Love beads hung around their necks. They wore bell-bottom blue jeans and ponchos. They went barefoot and wore tie-dyed T-shirts in bright colors and swirling patterns—the young women braless.

The hippie youth movement, however,

*The man's long hair and beads, and the woman's bare feet and flowered headband identify this 1967 couple as hippies. They are shown awaiting a jazz concert in San Francisco's Golden Gate Park.*

## Make love not war.

was much more than just a fashion style. It was a way of thinking and behaving. Hippies referred to most adults and figures of authority, including community and government leaders, as "the establishment." This generation of flower children was antiestablishment—they rejected the American way of life that had been so much a part of the fabric of society in the 1950s and early 1960s. They felt that their parents were slaves to society's expectations. They got married, worked for big business, and raised children in middle-class neighborhoods. Hippies, however, viewed their parents' materialistic values as meaningless. Instead, they promoted personal freedom— freedom to experience sexual relationships without being married and to use drugs to gain greater understanding of themselves. Hippies also opposed political aggression, and many ignored the laws that required men to register for military service. "Make love not war," they chanted. U.S. soldiers had been fighting Communist forces in a small country in Southeast Asia called Vietnam. Hippies opposed the Vietnam War (1957–1975).

During the summer of 1967, the media descended upon Haight-Ashbury (a neighborhood in San Francisco) to photograph and write feature stories about the new generation of flower children. The female flower children were not teenyboppers. And they certainly weren't Mouseketeers. Of the thousands of teenage girls who came to San Francisco in the summer of 1967, many were runaways searching for adventure. They were dropouts—from school, routine, boring jobs, or their parents' lifestyles.

Tourists, too, came to San Francisco that summer to gawk at the barefoot flower children sitting cross-legged on sidewalks and against storefronts, smoking marijuana and strumming guitars. Record companies came and fashion designers too. Soon love beads and tied-dyed T-shirts were on sale in stores across the United States. Just as the Gidget sensation had swept across the country a decade earlier, the hippie movement of the late 1960s had become a cultural phenomenon. Even some adults adopted the hairstyles and casual clothing. Soon it wasn't just the gentle people anymore who were wearing tie-dyed T-shirts and flowers in their hair.

# CHAPTER FOUR
# CIVIL RIGHTS
# AND WRONGS

*Thousands of Americans march near the U.S. Capitol at a civil rights rally on August 28, 1963.*

*I have learned over the years that when one's mind is made up, this diminishes fear; knowing what must be done does away with fear.*

—Rosa Parks in her book *Quiet Strength* (1994)

# IN 1951 LINDA BROWN, AN AFRICAN AMERICAN

girl, was a third-grade student in Topeka, Kansas. At that time, many schools in the United States, especially in southern states, were segregated by race. The closest elementary school to Linda Brown's home was just seven blocks away, but it was a school for white children only. Linda could not attend. She had a dangerous walk through a railroad yard to get to the school for African American children. Her father sued the school district in Topeka for the right to send his daughter to the closer school. School officials resisted, and the case went to court. Three years later, on May 17, 1954, the U.S. Supreme Court ruled in the *Brown v. Board of Education of Topeka* case. The decision was unanimously in favor of Brown. Chief Justice Earl Warren stated that separate schools for black and white children could not ensure an equal education. The Supreme Court decision legally ended school segregation. Enforcing the law, however, would prove to be a violent chapter in U.S. history.

## Women Make News, 1957— ELIZABETH ECKFORD GOES TO CENTRAL HIGH

A Supreme Court decision is an important document. But the challenge of integrating U.S. schools fell upon a few brave individuals. One of those individuals was fifteen-year-old Elizabeth Eckford from Little Rock, Arkansas.

Elizabeth Eckford wanted to become a lawyer. Little Rock Central High School offered a speech course that her school did not. During the summer of 1957, Elizabeth told her parents of her decision to transfer to all-white Central High. They were against it. It was too dangerous. But Elizabeth insisted. She was not the only African American high school student who would attempt to integrate the high school that fall. With the encouragement of the National Association for the Advancement of Colored People, which wished to implement the recent *Brown v. Board of Education* decision that had made school segregation illegal, eight other students had also applied for transfers. Elizabeth, however, would be the first to encounter a mob.

The school superintendent had warned the African American students that they would be called names. He also advised their parents not to accompany their children to school, as that might incite violence among the protesters who were sure to gather for the first day of school. The plan was that all nine children would meet and walk into the school together. But at the last minute, those plans changed. The leaders of the local NAACP chapter, including white and black religious ministers, decided to

*Teenager Elizabeth Eckford is pursued by menacing white parents as she is turned away from entering Little Rock Central High School by the Arkansas National Guard in 1957. The guard was acting under the orders of Governor Orval Faubus.*

take the students to the school in a car. Elizabeth's family, however, did not have a telephone, so they never got the message.

The first morning of school, Elizabeth was more excited than nervous. She wanted to make a good impression and had sewn a new dress with a full skirt to wear. She pulled on her white bobby socks, donned a pair of sunglasses, and grabbed a spiral notebook. Before she left the house, she said good-bye to her mother and she prayed.

Meanwhile, a crowd of white men and women, furious at being forced to integrate their schools, were gathering on the sidewalks and street in front of Central High School. The governor of Arkansas had ordered the state's National Guard to surround the school. They arrived that morning in jeeps and trucks. Their weapons for

riot control included rifles with fixed bayonets and tear gas canisters. They, too, were waiting when Elizabeth walked down the street, alone.

"Two, four, six, eight," the crowd began to chant, "We ain't gonna integrate."

Elizabeth's knees began to tremble, but she walked on. She glanced around for a friendly face among the hundreds of people. An older woman spat at her. As Elizabeth neared the entrance of Central High, she saw a white girl walk past the soldier and into the school. When Elizabeth stepped forward, however, he blocked her path. Elizabeth thought perhaps she had gone to the wrong door. So she walked farther down the street to another door. Here, too, soldiers blocked her way. The main entrance was just a little farther, and she walked on. This time the soldiers blocked her entrance by raising and crossing their guns across their chests.

Panic seized her as she realized the National Guard was not there to protect her. They were there to keep her out. One soldier pointed to the street where the mob began to surge forward toward her. They cursed her. They called her "nigger" and "bitch." Someone shouted, "Lynch her! Lynch her!" Students from Central High stood by. Some jeered along with the adults. Others felt frightened and ashamed, but not one stepped forward to help.

Terrified, Elizabeth glanced down the street toward a bus stop. There was no reason to think that the bench there could provide safety, but she had nowhere else to go. She started walking in that direction. The mob followed her, still cursing and jeering.

Somehow she made it to the bench. A white man sat down beside her. "I'm a reporter for the *New York Times*," he told her. "May I have your name?"

She didn't answer. Tears ran down her cheeks.

The reporter was Benjamin Fine, a man who had predicted that juvenile delinquency would destroy society if parents didn't control their children. That morning in Little Rock, Arkansas, it was the parents who were out of control. Later, Benjamin Fine would say that Elizabeth reminded him of his own teenage daughter and that was why he put his arm around her shoulder and said, "Don't let them see you cry." John Chancellor, a reporter for NBC television, watched from a distance, fearing that the crowd would murder an innocent child. He, too, was frightened—for her but also for himself and his country. And then an older white woman pushed her way forward. She shouted at the others, "She's scared. She's just a

> "She's scared. She's just a little girl. Six months from now you'll be ashamed at what you're doing."
>
> —Grace Lorch, referring to Elizabeth Eckford, 1957

little girl. Six months from now you'll be ashamed at what you're doing." Elizabeth understood that someone was helping her, but she was so frightened that she did not understand what the woman, Grace Lorch, was saying. Together Lorch and the *New York Times* reporter helped Elizabeth across the street. The mob still seethed nearby, and Lorch reportedly shouted, "I'm just waiting for one of you to touch me! I'm just aching to punch somebody in the nose."

When the bus arrived, Lorch stepped aboard with the teenager and rode with her to the School for the Blind, where Elizabeth's mother worked. Once there, in her mother's arms, Elizabeth broke down and cried.

Elizabeth's photograph and Grace Lorch's too appeared in newspapers across the country. Television broadcasts also showed Elizabeth's controlled behavior while others around her sneered and threatened. *Time* magazine reported that a soldier protectively escorted the terrified teenager from the school entrance to the bench at the bus stop. But that was not how the reporter from the *New York Times* remembered it. Nor was it what John Chancellor had witnessed.

Elizabeth returned to the high school the next day and each day after, until at last the nine black transfer students gained admittance to the school. Integration happened only after President Dwight D. Eisenhower intervened and sent the National Guard to Little Rock.

Civil rights was not a woman's issue only. It affected Americans of all races, young and old, male and female. The media image of Elizabeth Eckford, however, showed the country that a young woman could face frightening adversity with dignity. Elizabeth Eckford took a stand against social injustice. The image and her story became part of U.S. history. The media and textbooks discussing the civil rights movement frequently reprinted the image. It is impossible to know how many other young women saw

> The media image of Elizabeth Eckford showed the country that a young woman could face frightening adversity with dignity.

Elizabeth's image in the newspaper in 1957 and afterward. No doubt, many who did found courage to make a stand of their own.

Years later, *Ebony* magazine published an article titled "100 Most Fascinating Black Women of the 20th Century."

# Women Make News, 1961—
# CHARLAYNE HUNTER ATTENDS THE UNIVERSITY OF GEORGIA

On the day that Grace Lorch helped rescue Elizabeth Eckford from a mob that threatened to lynch her, she predicted that in six months those same furious women and men would be ashamed of their behavior. She was wrong. It took much longer than a few months. For years more, violent conflicts over integration exploded in other schools in other cities and states. In 1961 Charlayne Hunter was the first African American female student to enroll in the University of Georgia in Athens. If a fellow student harassed her on the campus, other students would approach her and bolster her spirits.

Then came the basketball game and Georgia's loss to its archrival. Frustrated students turned toward the dormitory where Hunter lived. Almost one thousand students stormed the steps of the building. Some threw bricks that smashed her windows. The local police used tear gas to disperse the mob. The school expelled Hunter, supposedly for her own safety. Her dismissal suggested that Hunter had violated the school's rules of conduct or that she had failed to succeed in her studies. She had not. *Time* magazine reported that the young coed left the university that night in tears. She would later return and complete her education. She became the first African American woman to graduate from the University of Georgia, in 1963. She would later become an internationally respected journalist.

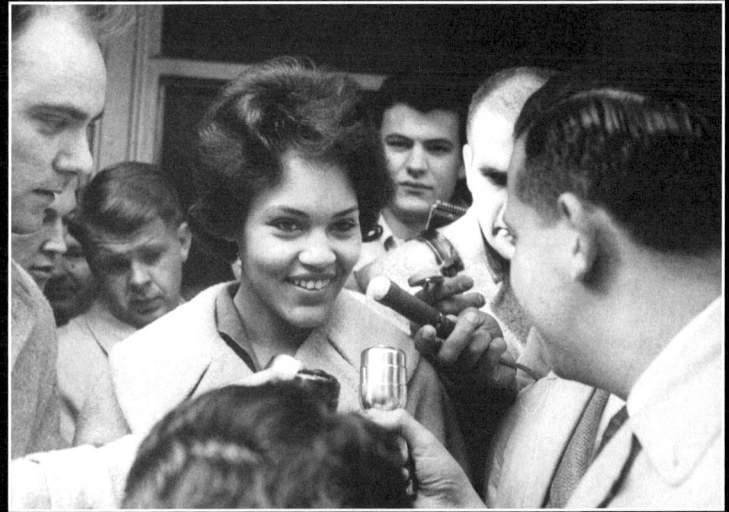

*Charlayne Hunter was one of the first two African Americans to register for admission at the University of Georgia, only to be driven away by demonstrating fellow students. She needed a court order and body guards for readmission. She is shown at left leaving the campus after registering as a student.*

Included on this list were artists, writers, and activists. It named singer Lena Horne, writer Maya Angelou, educator Mary McLeod Bethune, and journalist Ida B. Wells-Barnett. On that same list was Elizabeth Eckford. "They are . . . unforgettable," wrote *Ebony* of the women. "They attracted and held national attention, delighting us and challenging us and making us bigger."

## THE OTHER AMERICAN DREAM

When the curtain fell in the Ethel Barrymore Theater in New York City on March 11, 1959, the audience in the theater understood that they had just experienced a story unlike any other on Broadway. By the time the enthusiastic applause ended and the house lights came up, the playwright Lorraine Hansberry had become an overnight sensation.

Hansberry's play *A Raisin in the Sun* told the story of the Younger family, three generations living in a crowded slum building on the South Side of Chicago, Illinois. Lena Younger receives a ten-thousand-dollar insurance payment after the death of her husband. Her son, a chauffeur to a white family, wants her to give him the money so he can invest in a liquor store. Lena has other ideas. She puts a down payment on a house in a Chicago suburb. But there is a problem. The Youngers will be the first African American family to live in the neighborhood.

Lorraine Hansberry based the play partly on her childhood experiences with racism. Born in Chicago in 1930, she confronted the rage of racism when she was just seven years old. Her father had moved his family into an all-white neighborhood. She remembered very clearly the

*Lorraine Hansberry's* A Raisin in the Sun *was the first play written by an African American woman to be produced on Broadway. The work received the New York Drama Critics' Circle Award, making Hansberry* (above) *the youngest playwright as well as the first African American to ever receive the award.*

*Claudia McNeil and Sidney Poitier are shown in a scene from Lorraine Hansberry's* A Raisin in the Sun. *The two actors starred in the original 1959 Broadway production for which they were both nominated for Tony Awards, as well as in the 1961 film version.*

rocks that came through the windows of her home, thrown by angry white neighbors. Her father sued for the right to live in that community, and he won.

"I was born black and female," Hansberry would later write in her autobiography. Those two factors could have become roadblocks to her success as a writer, but she did not accept the belief of the times that African Americans—and especially female African Americans— could not become playwrights. As an aspiring writer, she thought the African American characters she saw in movies and on television were stereotypes. She was just twenty-eight years old when she wrote *A Raisin in the Sun*. She told her mother that she wanted to show white Americans that black Americans had strengths and flaws just like anyone else. "I think [the play] will help a lot of people to understand how we are just as complicated as they are—and just as mixed up—but above all, that we have among our . . . ranks people who are the very essence of human dignity." The play's only white character is Karl Lindner. He visits the Youngers with a bribe. He and his neighbors are willing to purchase the house from Lena Younger, to keep the neighborhood segregated. He tries to reason with her.

Negro families, he tells her, were happier when they lived among their own people. As the play ends, the Younger family has refused the white community's bribe. They will move into their new home whatever the consequences.

A *Raisin in the Sun* was controversial. In addition to the playwright being black and female, the actors and the director were also African American. "You can't do that on Broadway," people told Philip Rose, the play's producer. Rose was a friend of Hansberry and believed her play could make theater history. Rose, who was white, struggled to raise money to rent the theater, build the set, and hire the actors.

On opening night, Philip Rose and Lorraine Hansberry sat next to each other in the fourth row. Every seat in the theater had sold, a good sign. Still, the producer and the playwright were nervous. How would this audience of both black and white theatergoers react? At one point, Rose noticed a white man leave his seat. He noticed that on either side of this man sat African American couples. The man did not leave the theater, however. He stood in the back, and once the curtain fell, he applauded too. The gesture indicated, at least to Rose, that Hansberry's message had meaning for white audiences as well as for African Americans.

That night, once all the theatergoers had left the building, Rose asked the young playwright to join him to celebrate at the exclusive restaurant Sardi's. Hansberry reluctantly agreed. When she entered the restaurant, most of the people there were white. They turned their heads and stared. Then they gave her a standing ovation.

The New York Drama Critics' Circle also praised Hansberry's play, giving *A Raisin in the Sun* the award for best play of the year. Being black and female could have limited what Lorraine Hansberry achieved. Instead, her race and her sex gave her a unique perspective on the American dream. White people who saw *A Raisin in the Sun* left the theater with a new understanding of the frustration and anger that minorities felt at being denied the American dream of owning a home in a safe neighborhood.

## DAYS OF HOPE, DAYS OF HORROR

Fannie Lou Hamer had been a sharecropper in Mississippi for most of her life. She was a U.S. citizen, but she did not vote in the 1960 presidential election. To vote, a person had to register with the local government. Although voting is a right guaranteed by the Constitution, in 1960 hundreds of thousands of African Americans—both women and men—had not registered to vote. Some did not know how. Others were afraid. In some southern states, racist people threatened to harm African Americans who attempted to register. The Constitution does not require that voters be able to read and write. Yet some local government leaders required African Americans to pass a literacy test before registering their names on the list of eligible voters.

Fannie Lou Hamer went to a meeting organized by the civil rights group known as the Student Nonviolent Coordinating Committee (SNCC), where she learned that black people had the right to vote. When the white farmer on whose land she worked learned that Hamer had registered to vote, he gave her a choice: either she remove her name from the voter list or lose her job. "We are not ready for that in Mississippi," he told her, meaning he did not want African Americans to have voting power. Hamer did not remove her name, so she lost her job and her home on the white farmer's land. A few weeks later, night riders (white men on horses who terrorized African Americans) fired shots into the house where she and her husband had gone to live.

In June 1963, Hamer attended a voter registration workshop, helping other African Americans learn how to register. While she was traveling home, police arrested her. In the county jail, one of the white guards told Hamer, "We are going to make sure you wish you was dead." In a cell, the guards ordered her to lie on her stomach. They then forced another African American prisoner to beat her with a leather club.

Despite the beating, Fannie Lou Hamer could not be silenced. In 1964 she traveled to Atlantic City, New Jersey, to speak at the Democratic Party's national convention. Delegates at this convention

*On August 22, 1964, Fanny Lou Hamer spoke before the Democratic National Convention in Atlantic City, New Jersey. Her goal was to win the right for her integrated political party—the Freedom Democratic Party—to represent Mississippi at the national convention that year.*

had been elected by their states to represent the voters and elect a candidate for president of the United States. In Mississippi the Democratic Party had blocked the election of African American delegates. So Hamer became one of the founders of the Mississippi Democratic Freedom Party, an alternative party open to black and white delegates.

At the national convention, most of the delegates were white and male. Fannie Lou Hamer spoke to the convention of the harassment she and other African Americans endured in Mississippi. In the days that followed, she met with delegates, including Senator Walter Mondale of Minnesota, who would one day become vice president of the United States and run unsuccessfully for president. She insisted that African Americans—male and female—had a right to become delegates. Partly as a result of her fight for justice, the Democratic Party passed a resolution. It would not accept any delegate to the convention who had been chosen on the basis of racial discrimination. "When you hear people say that citizens can't do anything, that it is foolish to become involved," Mondale would later tell the press, "please tell them to take a hard look at American history, and while you're at it, take a look at Fannie Lou Hamer as well."

"When you hear people say that citizens can't do anything, that it is foolish to become involved, please tell them to take a hard look at American history, and while you're at it, take a look at Fannie Lou Hamer as well."

—Senator Walter Mondale, 1964

## ROSA PARKS AND THE REVEREND KING MARCH ON WASHINGTON, D.C.

Although women were actively involved in civil rights organizations of the 1950s and 1960s, men were the primary decision makers in those

*Civil rights history maker Rosa Parks was not allowed to join the men at the front of the March on Washington on August 28, 1963. That day Martin Luther King Jr. (third from left, front row) gave his famous "I have a dream" speech in front of the Lincoln Memorial.*

organizations. Women could type letters and print copies of stirring speeches to pass out on street corners. However, the speakers in front of the microphones were more often than not men. Women could cook food for the workers and clean the meeting rooms, but they could not run a meeting. The news media spotlighted these male leaders but rarely turned the camera lens on the women who also participated. This was the case in August of 1963 during a peaceful mass protest, a march on Washington, D.C. Thousands of men and women, both black and white, attended. At the head of the march with arms linked were the Reverend Martin Luther King Jr. and other male leaders of the civil rights movement.

Eight years earlier, in 1955, an African American woman, Rosa Parks. had refused to give up her seat on a bus to a white passenger, violating a city law. Her arrest triggered the Montgomery, Alabama, bus boycott and set in motion additional civil rights demonstrations. Although Parks marched on Washington in 1963, she did not walk alongside or even immediately behind King. The organizers of the march told her to walk with the other women farther back. Nor did the organizers invite Parks or any women, in fact, to speak during the demonstration.

"Nowadays, women wouldn't stand for being kept so much in the background," Rosa Parks would later say, "but back then women's rights hadn't become a popular cause yet."

## WEDNESDAY'S WOMEN

In addition to racism, black women had their own list of civil rights and wrongs they wished to focus on: unequal pay, unequal employment opportunities, and sexual harassment. The men silenced them and elbowed their issues to the sidelines. Women's equality wasn't considered as important as the primary goal of the civil rights workers—the right of all African American citizens to register to vote.

Some women formed their own organizations or took measures independently of the larger civil rights groups. During the summer of 1964, women from northern cities, including Boston, New York, Chicago, and Saint Paul, traveled to Mississippi. There they met with southern women to learn more about one another and to ease racial tensions. The meetings were interracial, meaning white and black women from both the northern states and Mississippi sat together. They called their project Wednesdays in Mississippi.

Teams of white and African American women arrived in Mississippi every week on Tuesdays. They spent Wednesdays visiting voter registration offices and Freedom Schools, classrooms set up for African American children to

*Dorothy Height* (right), *founder of Wednesdays in Mississippi, has a cup of tea with Polly Cowan, the group's executive director. In 1964 the group began to send interracial and interfaith teams of northern women to Mississippi to offer support to their southern sisters. Eventually that support came to include educational resources and professional training.*

gain not only academic knowledge but also the skills they would need to work in the civil rights movement. The women also experienced firsthand the poverty and injustice of segregated communities. Marian Wright Edelman, a young African American lawyer from Boston, said that the Wednesdays in Mississippi group "had a transforming effect. Many white women really began to see that what they believed [about race relations] was not true."

Because Mississippi was the most segregationist state in the South, the organization had chosen the state for its integrated meetings. Many white people there resisted civil rights for blacks. Some whites still used beatings, rapes, and lynchings to terrorize and control African Americans in Mississippi.

Some women who went to Mississippi were members of women's groups, such as the National Council of Jewish Women, the League of Women Voters, and the National Council of Negro Women. Some were college professors. Polly Cowan, who founded the project with Dorothy Height, called the women the Cadillac Crowd because they were socially prominent. Many of their husbands held leadership positions in industry and business. The women might have worn hats, gloves, and pearl necklaces, said Goodwillie Steadman, one of the Wednesday women, but they had nerves of steel. Many of the northern women had not traveled South before. And most had not experienced the fear and intimidation of segregated communities—where public toilets and water foundations were labeled Whites Only or Coloreds Only. The women often kept their travel plans secret. "My husband would kill me if he knew I were here," said one white woman.

The women, especially the African American women, risked physical harm at the hands of local white supremacists for meeting as an interracial group. So the women did not protest or carry signs. They wore white gloves like most southern women did. The black women roomed separately from the white women, and while they met together as a group, those meetings were in secret. In public the women were careful not to be seen speaking to one another.

The secret project, however, increased awareness of the challenges communities faced in trying to integrate. Once the northern women returned home—to be replaced by another team of racial ambassadors the following Tuesday—they spoke about their experiences with other women's groups.

"Fear is still the most important stumbling block to progress," stated the final report of Wednesdays in Mississippi. Women willing to overcome their fears were the first step in building a bridge of understanding.

# DAUGHTERS OF BILITIS "COME OUT"

In the 1950s and 1960s, some women fought for a different type of civil rights—the right to love whomever they chose, even if that other person was also a woman. Many in society, including medical doctors and psychologists, believed that homosexuality, either in males or females, was a disease. As a result, many lesbians kept their physical attractions to members of the same sex a secret. Two women, in particular, decided to fight for the rights of homosexuals.

Del Martin and Phyllis Lyon founded the nation's first lesbian organization, the Daughters of Bilitis (DOB), in San Francisco in 1955. Only eight members strong, its stated mission was to improve the status of lesbians through public education and to provide lesbians with a way of meeting one another and spending time together. The group grew rapidly, opening chapters in dozens of U.S. cities. The organization's national newsletter, *The Ladder*, published articles on events of the time, as well as poetry and short stories. Some articles discussed the fears and social stigmas lesbians experienced, which included loss of jobs and removal of their children

*DOB founders Del Martin* (right) *and Phyllis Lyon* (left) *have been active in the National Organization for Women* (NOW) *since 1967, working toward the acceptance of lesbian issues as feminist issues.*

from their care. An issue of *The Ladder* published in 1957 showed a woman removing a mask. The message was that lesbians need not hide their true identities. The phrase "coming out" became associated with a woman admitting that she was a lesbian. As author Marcia Gallo put it, "*The Ladder* was a lifeline, . . . a means of expressing and sharing otherwise private thoughts, . . . of breaking through isolation and fear."

During the late 1950s and 1960s, the DOB joined with the predominantly male Mattachine Society. Beset by political divisions—mainly having to do with the female members' loyalties being divided between gay rights and women's rights—the melded group folded in 1970. But it left a legacy for both sexes as a precursor to the gay liberation movement that flourished in later decades. Lesbian feminists went on to become an important factor in the 1970s second wave of feminism—albeit not without some stumbling blocks put in place by their straight sisters in the National Organization of Women (NOW).

## HELP WANTED: MALE, HELP WANTED: FEMALE

The civil rights movement focused on eliminating discrimination against minorities. Women were not a minority in the United States, and yet they also experienced discrimination.

If a woman wanted to find a job, she might have looked first in the classified ads in her local newspaper. Newspapers sorted job openings into one of two categories: male and female. Among the jobs listed under Help Wanted: Male might be mechanic, electrician, truck driver, or TV serviceman. Among those listed under Help Wanted: Female were usually waitress, secretary, nurse's aide, and salesclerk. One woman who read the want ads in the 1960s concluded, "All the good jobs were for men and all the dead-end jobs for women."

For many years, Esther Peterson had worked as a labor activist. She fought for better wages and safer conditions for working women, especially those who worked in factories. In 1961 President Kennedy appointed her the assistant secretary of labor and director of the Women's Bureau. She began working on a new project for the president, the Presidential Commission on the Status of Women.

*Esther Peterson, shown here in 1960, was assistant secretary of labor and director of the United States Women's Bureau for President John F. Kennedy. The Women's Bureau was established in 1920 to improve conditions and opportunities for wage-earning women.*

"Eleanor (Roosevelt) taught us you could do things; she helped lead the way. (Women) stopped licking stamps and started getting into the decision-making."

—Esther Peterson, 1995

Peterson believed in putting herself in other people's shoes. As a labor activist, she often visited the homes and workplaces of working women. She met with the women face-to-face. "I'll never forget going to a Bendix factory," Peterson said, "and here was a big husky woman lifting a box from one conveyor belt onto another one. And this man was standing by her. And I said, 'Why doesn't he do it?' And she said, 'He's not strong enough. I'm stronger and I can do it.' And then, Peterson said, preparing to deliver the punch line, I found that she got 15 cents an hour less than he did. By golly, did that give me the ammunition I needed to work on." Peterson's strategy was simple. First, get the facts firsthand. Second, fight back.

Fifteen women and eleven men served on the commission with Peterson. Former First Lady Eleanor Roosevelt was the chairperson. "Eleanor taught us you could do things; she helped lead the way," said Peterson. "[Women] stopped just licking the stamps and started getting into the decision-making."

After two years of study and eleven hundred pages of notes and correspondence, the commission published its report, titled simply *American Women*. It documented many unfair labor practices that had a negative effect on women. Women were promoted less often and earned less money than men, even when they did the same job. It wasn't a matter of a few pennies either. A man might earn one dollar an hour, while women who did the same job earned just fifty-nine to sixty-four cents. There were other discriminatory practices as well. Employers generally gave women less life and health insurance and fewer retirement benefits than they gave men. Labor practices often prevented women from working overtime to earn extra money. Some employers fired women once they married or became pregnant.

As a result of this report, Congress passed the Equal Pay Act of 1963. It became against the law to pay women less than men for doing the same job. Enforcing the law, however, would not prove so easy.

## SEX AND TITLE VII

The civil rights movement of the 1950s and early 1960s had made Americans aware of social injustices experienced by African Americans. In 1963 President Kennedy presented to Congress a draft of the Civil Rights bill, known as Title VII. As written, Title VII outlawed discrimination on the basis of race, color, religion, or national origin. Representative Howard Smith of Virginia was a segregationist.

# A SMILE AND A HANDSHAKE

The Peace Corps was a different kind of army. At a time when civil rights struggles were pulling apart the country, the Peace Corps recruited young people of all races, women as well as men. President Kennedy created the program to build understanding between the United States and other nations and to promote world peace. Volunteers had to pass an examination and undergo training, which might include anything from learning another language to learning how to pluck a chicken. In addition to meals and housing, volunteers received two dollars a day while in training. Once assigned to a host nation, they received no pay other than the satisfaction of serving their country and the world. They lived among the local people. They ate the same food as the locals and drank the same water, sometimes contaminated.

In 1961 the U.S. military did not allow women to enlist as soldiers. Women in general and women of color in particular faced prejudice and career limitations in the United States. The Peace Corps welcomed them to apply their intelligence and talents to a challenging job.

*President Kennedy greets Peace Corps volunteers on the White House lawn in August 1962. By 1963 the two-year-old program had seventy-three hundred volunteers serving in forty-four countries. The number of volunteers more than doubled by 1966.*

He did not support civil rights for African Americans. He did not wish to see schools and neighborhoods integrated in his state. Furthermore, he believed a government couldn't outlaw an attitude or social behavior.

To kill the bill, Representative Smith proposed adding the word *sex* to the language of Title VII. The reaction in Congress to his proposed amendment was uproarious laughter, observed Congresswoman Martha Griffiths. Congress was predominantly male. While many of those politicians believed racism was a social injustice, they did not think sex discrimination was. Perhaps some doubted sex discrimination even existed.

The laughter stopped, however, when Griffiths stood to speak. Were women second-class citizens? The men's laughter just then, she said, had proved that they were. The bill, as written, would protect African Americans, including women, she argued. But it would not, as written, protect white women. Could Congress give civil rights to African American women and not all women? Any man who refused to vote against adding the word *sex* to Title VII was voting against his wife, daughter, and mother, she said.

Although Smith had hoped adding the word *sex* to Title VII would defeat the civil rights bill, that didn't happened. On July 2, 1964, Title VII became law, outlawing discrimination on the basis of race, color, religion, national origin . . . and sex. The United States would never be the same again.

*Martha Wright Griffiths stands in front of the U.S. Capitol Building in 1962. She had served in the U.S. House of Representatives since 1954 and was the first woman to ever serve on the influential House Committee on Ways and Means. She worked diligently and successfully for including the prohibition of sex discrimination under Title VII of the Civil Rights Act of 1964. This legislation propelled the women's movement forward in the following decades.*

# A FIRST LADY'S LESSON IN GRIEF

On the morning of November 22, 1963, First Lady Jackie Kennedy dressed in a pink suit, matching pink pillbox hat, blue shoes, stockings, and white gloves. She and President John F. Kennedy were in Texas for a political appearance. At approximately twelve thirty, the slow-moving motorcade turned onto Elm Street. The Kennedys were waving to the crowds along the street. Then gunshots exploded. The first shot struck the president. A second shot and then a third cracked. The president fell sideways into his wife's lap. Within seconds, the limousine driver was speeding toward Parkland Hospital. Vice President Lyndon Johnson and his wife, Lady Bird, unharmed, were riding in a different car. At Parkland Hospital, Lady Bird Johnson remembered getting out of her car and looking over her shoulder. She would later write in her diary what she saw: "In the president's car, a bundle of pink, just like a drift of blossoms, lying on the back seat. It was Mrs. Kennedy lying over the President's body."

The president died a short time later.

In the days that followed, Jacqueline Kennedy's dignity as the widowed First Lady comforted a nation. She appeared on the steps of the White House, dressed in black. She held the hands of her children, Caroline on one side and John Jr. on the other. Perhaps her most controversial decision was to walk behind her husband's casket in the funeral procession from the White House to Saint Matthew's Cathedral. The Secret Service felt that her exposure to the public was too dangerous. President Lyndon Johnson and dignitaries from around the world, including the president of France, had also vowed to walk with her. She insisted. Her decision sent a message to the world that the United States would not hide from those who threaten, terrorize, or kill.

*Jacqueline Kennedy receives the flag that covered her husband's coffin, November 25, 1963.*

# CHAPTER FIVE

# Women Warriors of the Cold War

For my Mother's Day gift this year,
I don't want candy or flowers.
I want an end to killing.

We who have given life
Must be dedicated to preserving it.
Please talk peace.

—Another Mother for Peace campaign, 1967

*Women Strike for Peace supporters march from the Capitol to the White House in Washington, D.C., on December 13, 1962.*

# Soon after the end of World War II,

in the summer of 1946, the U.S. military conducted an atomic test called Operation Crossroads. They exploded two atomic bombs on the small island of Bikini in the South Pacific. The military knew the power of the bombs, having seen the horrific destruction of the Japanese cities of Hiroshima and Nagasaki the year before. An atomic explosion creates a large fireball, which vaporizes everything at the point of explosion. An intense heat follows the blast, searing metal as well as human flesh. The explosion creates another killing effect—radiation. Radiation in the bomb's mushroom cloud rises into the atmosphere and eventually drifts down again. Many people who survived the explosions in Hiroshima and Nagasaki died weeks or months later. They had been poisoned by the fine radioactive dust particles.

## From Operation Crossroads to Operation Alert

Initially, only the United States knew how to build superatomic weapons. But that knowledge was incomplete. What were the health effects of atomic blasts on living creatures? If another country were to develop atomic weapons, how could the United States best defend itself? These were the questions Operation Crossroads hoped to answer.

The military had spent many months planning this test. They invited news reporters from around the world to come to Bikini to witness the explosions. Anchored in the lagoon were various navy ships, including aircraft carriers, cruisers, battleships, and even a submarine. Tethered on the decks of some ships were goats, sheep, and pigs. When the countdown began, all military personnel and all journalists were safely aboard ships approximately 18 miles (29 kilometers) away. They waited with binoculars, notebooks, and cameras.

Overhead, a military plane approached and dropped the first bomb on Bikini. A *Washington Post* reporter who witnessed the explosion from his ship described the first two killing effects of the bomb: the blast was "a fearsome blaze of light." The heat wave was "a giant rumble" that rocked his ship even miles away. "A creamy canopy of cloud, tinged with pink writhed and twisted five miles [8 km] high," he wrote. The rising mushroom cloud "looked as though a giant mountain had risen from the sea, as though we were watching the formation of a continent," wrote a reporter for the *New York Times*.

Each atomic explosion creates radioactive fallout. This fallout is a very fine dust of chemicals, including uranium and strontium. The military understood that this rain of chemicals could make the air and the water

The rising mushroom cloud "looked as though a giant mountain had risen from the sea, as though we were watching the formation of a continent,"

—a reporter for the *New York Times* reporting on a nuclear test in 1946

poisonous. A reporter could describe the blast and heat of the atomic explosion. But the reporter had no words for the fallout, simply because it was not visible. It did not flash, thunder, or rock the ship. No one, not even the military, knew for certain how dangerous the fallout might be or how long the air and water of the lagoon might remain radioactive (contaminated by radiation).

Within hours a strong northwest wind had swept away the towering mushroom cloud. The military returned to the lagoon. The heat of the atomic blast had melted the metal of many of the ships in the lagoon. Many of the test animals aboard these ships had died or were badly burned by the blast. Others, however, had survived and seemed normal. The military transported these animals back to laboratories in the United States. Within months, all the animals died.

When a nuclear bomb explodes, its radioactive cloud can travel in the upper atmosphere around the globe. Its fallout can rain on any town or city in any country. Could fallout contaminate the lakes and rivers from which people got their drinking water? Could it seep into the ground and contaminate the plants farmers grew? Scientists did not yet know the answers to these questions. Yet both the United States and the Soviet Union continued the

The publishers of the Buffalo Evening News *took* Operation Alert *very seriously, publishing an actual emergency edition of their paper. The masthead notes that the edition was compiled by a group of* News *employees who escaped because they were off duty or on vacation. They made their way back to perform this public service.*

*Many families of the 1950s built or purchased their own fallout shelters, stocking them with about two weeks worth of food and water. By the end of the 1960s, international treaties calmed fears of nuclear attack.*

aboveground testing of nuclear weapons throughout the 1950s.

To protect the Americans from an atomic attack, the U.S. government created a civil defense program called Operation Alert. During practice sessions, when an air-raid siren began to signal an attack, all people were to take cover, either in the basements of their homes or in public fallout shelters that were usually underground. Those who did not obey this order could be fined one hundred dollars, arrested, and sentenced to a year in prison.

Very likely, Mary Sharmat knew little about the atomic testing on Bikini. But she believed that if an atomic bomb exploded over New York City, the city would become a desert. "I felt that nuclear air-raid drills taught fear and hate towards an enemy," she said. Sharmat did not think of herself as a warrior maiden. Still, what she was about to do required warrior-like courage. She was going to break the law, a law she did not believe in.

One morning in 1959, Sharmat dressed in a black-and-white-checked cotton suit. Her shoes and handbag were red. She dressed her baby boy, Jimmy, in a blue linen outfit. She wanted to look like a sensible, respectable woman, she said. Perhaps she had chosen red, white, and blue for another reason—to express her patriotism. Before she left home, she had cooked a roast beef dinner for her husband. If she were arrested—and she fully expected to be—then her husband would still have something to eat. She had even packed an overnight bag for herself and her baby.

Sharmat put her son in his stroller and walked two blocks from her home in New York City. At the center island of Broadway and Eighty-sixth Street was a bench. She sat down. Nearby was a civil defense truck. She had known it would be there. She looked at her watch. In fifteen minutes, her rebellious act would begin. "I . . . gritted my teeth in determination not to become a coward and return home," she said.

At noon the air-raid sirens began to wail. Civil defense wardens wearing white helmets appeared on the streets and ordered

> "I . . . gritted my teeth in determination not to become a coward and return home."
>
> —Mary Sharmat, 1959

people to take cover. Sharmat did not move. One of the wardens approached, shouting, "Operation Alert. Take cover!"

"I can't take shelter," she said. "I do not believe in this."

The warden threatened to call the police. Sharmat said that was fine with her. The sirens were screeching. Jimmy was crying. A police officer approached Sharmat. "Lady," he said, "We're going to give you a ticket." She did not argue with him. She just refused to take cover. At last, he walked away. He didn't give her a ticket or arrest her.

At twelve fifteen, the sirens stopped, replaced by an all-clear signal. People began emerging from the city shelters. Mary Sharmat walked home and put her baby in his crib for a nap.

In the late edition of the newspaper that day, Sharmat read an article about a woman named Janice Smith. She, too, had refused to obey the civil defense order. "All these drills do are scare birds, babies and old ladies. I will not raise my children to go underground," she said.

Sharmat was not alone.

# Marguerite Higgins Reports on War

On June 25, 1950, the Communist forces of North Korea invaded South Korea. The invaders' intent was to unite Korea into a single, Communist nation. In response to the Communist aggression in this land halfway around the world, the United States sent soldiers to defend South Korea. The *New York Herald Tribune* sent Marguerite Higgins to Korea to report on the Korean War (1950–1953). Within a few weeks, however, General Douglas MacArthur ordered her out of the country. War was no place for a woman, he charged. The soldiers' language was unfit for a lady. So was the sanitation. The military had no bathroom facilities for women.

"I'm not here as a woman," Higgins said. She was a war correspondent. She understood the dangers, but they were part of the job. She added, "Nobody worries about powder rooms in Korea." The *New York Herald Tribune* also fought for its reporter to return to Korea. Eventually, MacArthur gave in and cabled the newspaper: "The ban on women correspondents has been lifted. Marguerite Higgins held in highest esteem by everyone." She was too. "Maggie wears mud like other women wear makeup," said the soldiers on the front lines. Higgins was often there with them, under fire, wearing baggy pants, boots, and a military cap. A year later, Higgins would win journalism's highest award, the Pulitzer Prize, for her overseas reporting.

In the mid-1960s, after the Korean War ended, U.S. soldiers were once more shipping out to a remote country in Asia. The Communist government of North Vietnam was at war with the Republic of South Vietnam. The Soviet Union and China, both Communist nations, supported the North Vietnamese. U.S. troops fought alongside the South Vietnamese. And once more, Marguerite Higgins was off to war with her typewriter and duffel bag. This time, however, Higgins would not survive the war. She contracted a rare tropical disease from the bite of a sand flea and died in 1966.

*Marguerite Higgins* (far right), *Far East bureau chief of the* New York Herald Tribune, *is shown here in 1950 in the hold of a cargo plane en route from South Korea to Tokyo, Japan.*

# The "Peace March Gals"

Mary Sharmat would disobey the civil defense law again in 1960 and 1961. Each year more women joined the rebellion and not just in New York City. These women did not argue about the destructive power of atomic weapons. Instead, they protested the U.S. government's military policies of testing nuclear weapons and adding more of these weapons to its arsenal.

On November 1, 1961, women in approximately sixty cities across the country—women who did not know one another—removed their aprons, switched off their vacuum cleaners, and simply stopped working. Women who held jobs outside the home did not report for work. They had learned about the Women Strike for Peace (WSP) through their neighborhood networks, including the Parent-Teacher Association (PTA) and the League of Women Voters. Many telephoned their friends and alerted them to what was about to happen. This time the women did not sit on park benches while air-raid sirens wailed. They knocked on the doors of their local government leaders and demanded that they "End the Arms Race—Not the Human Race."

*Newsweek* reported the startling event, commenting first on the women's appearances: "They were perfectly ordinary looking women, with their share of good looks; they looked like the women you would see driving ranch wagons, or shopping at

> "End the Arms Race—
> Not the Human Race."
>
> —Women Strike for Peace placard, 1961

the village market, or attending PTA meetings . . . carrying placards, many wheeling baby buggies or strollers—they marched on city halls and Federal buildings to show their concern about nuclear fallout."

No one knows for certain just how many women went on the peace strike that day, but some women's groups estimated as many as fifty thousand. Why had so many housewives and mothers, as well as career women across the country, suddenly become warriors for peace? There were several reasons.

*In October 1962, Women Strike for Peace members picketed the UN's headquarters in New York City. Public protests by the group eventually achieved some success in the form of a 1963 ban on atmospheric testing of the hydrogen bomb.*

In the fifteen years since the atomic explosion at Bikini, scientists had learned quite a bit more about the long-term effects of radiation. What they learned was terribly frightening. Studies had linked radiation exposure to cancer. In case of nuclear attack, advised the civil defense pamphlets of the 1950s, people should cover their mouths with handkerchiefs to avoid breathing in the radioactive fallout. The government told its citizens that scrubbing in a good bath could remove the radioactive residue. But scientists argued that those strategies would not pre-vent radiation sickness. In the 1950s, civil defense writers told people to take cover in their basements or fallout shelters with enough food and water supplies to last two weeks. But scientists argued that the poisonous radioactivity lingered longer than just a few weeks. It rained down upon the Earth for months, even years following an explosion. It contaminated plants and streams and therefore food supplies. The radioactive chemical strontium 90 had been found in cow's milk. This chemical lodges in the bone, especially the growing bone tissue of children.

Throughout the 1950s, the popular media told women that their most important responsibility in life was to care for their families. In the minds of the women protesters, demanding an end to the nuclear arms race was caring for their families. If women truly were the architects of peace, as one magazine writer had claimed, then they wished to build a world without atomic bombs.

The *San Francisco Examiner* said the WSP were "well-meaning" but naive. The paper said that Communists spies were duping, or tricking the women. The Federal Bureau of Investigation (FBI) apparently thought the same thing, for the agency secretly began investigating the women protesters. In 1962 the U.S. Congress announced an investigation of its own into the WSP and named twelve women to appear before a committee for questioning.

The hearings lasted three days. During that time, every seat in the chamber was taken. Women had traveled from eleven states to attend and support the twelve women giving testimony. They brought their children so that the members of the congressional committee would be reminded why the women had struck for peace. Many women did not bother to hush their fussing children or stop them from crawling on the floor.

The committee called Blanche Posner, a retired schoolteacher from New York, as its first witness. When she stood, the entire room of women also stood. Chairperson Clyde Doyle banged his gavel, ordering the women to sit down. When the committee called its next witness, the women applauded. The chairperson banged his gavel again and outlawed applauding as well as standing. The women obeyed. A reporter described how the women reacted next: "Then

> The media told women that their most important responsibility in life was to care for their families. In the minds of the women protesters, demanding an end to the nuclear arms race was caring for their families.

*In December 1962, women and children packed the room as the House Un-American Activities Committee (HUAC) examined fourteen Women Strike for Peace activists. The press was amused. The* Washington Post *ran a cartoon showing a congressman asking his colleague if these people were subversive because they were for peace or because they were women.*

they took to running out to kiss the witness. . . . Finally, each woman as she was called was met and handed a huge bouquet. By then Doyle was a beaten man."

A committee member asked Dagmar Wilson if she was the leader of the WSP. The WSP wasn't a formal organization, she insisted. "Nobody controls anybody in the Women Strike for Peace. We're all leaders."

Newspapers around the country reported on the hearings. Editorial cartoons mocked the committee for taking on half a million angry American mothers. "Peace March Gals Make Red Hunters Look Silly," wrote Russell Baker in his newspaper column. The *Chicago Daily News* ran this headline: "It's

Ladies Day at the Capitol: Hoots, Howls—and Charm; Congressmen Meet Match."

The women were patriotic, the committee concluded. The three-day investigation had not revealed any Communist spies within their ranks. The investigation, however, had drawn national media attention to an issue thousands of American women felt passionately about. The WSP was partly responsible for the Limited Test Ban Treaty, signed both by the United States and the Soviet Union in 1963. The treaty didn't outlaw nuclear weapons. But it did prohibit testing nuclear weapons in the atmosphere, in outer space, and underwater. (Underground tests were still allowed.)

Although the women had triumphed, the WSP did not disband. On the horizon loomed another conflict that threatened the lives of their children—war in a small country in Southeast Asia called Vietnam. Once again, the WSP would march in protest.

## Women Make News, 1962: Rachel Carson's Silent Spring

Her friends called her Ray. Rachel Carson was a solemn, shy scientist who created a controversy in 1962 when she published her book *Silent Spring*. She began that book with a description of a spring morning in a small town in the heart of the United States, surrounded by farmlands, orchards, and woods. But this spring, the land was blighted. The grass and woods were burned brown. Flowers had not budded or bloomed. No birdsong was in the air because the birds had died. No fish swam in the streams because the fish had died. The farm animals—chickens, cattle, and sheep—had sickened and died. The townspeople were complaining of "mysterious maladies." Doctors had no idea what plague had descended upon the land. There was one clue, however. She wrote: "In the gutters under the eaves and between the shingles of the roofs, a white granular powder still showed a few patches; some weeks before it had fallen like snow upon the roofs and the lawns, the fields and streams."

*Rachel Carson is shown talking to lawmakers in 1963 about the dangers of pesticides.*

The readers of *Silent Spring* might have guessed that the mysterious sickness and sudden deaths were the result of an atomic bomb

—Rachel Carson, 1962

attack. But that wasn't what Rachel Carson was describing. The white granules were chemicals, and the people had poisoned themselves.

She titled that frightening opening chapter "A Fable for Tomorrow." But the rest of the book was not science fiction or fantasy. It was scientific fact.

Her research on the book had begun in 1958, when a friend wrote to her about a startling event. Large numbers of birds had died on Cape Cod in Massachusetts, after a widespread spraying of DDT, a pesticide. Was the use of poisonous chemicals to kill insects hazardous to the environment and to people? Her investigations took four years. "The more I learned about the use of pesticides, the more appalled I became," she said.

Since the end of World War II, the U.S. chemical industry had thrived. The chemicals used to kill weeds, insects, and pests had names difficult to pronounce: dieldrin, parathion, heptachlor, and malathion. To most Americans, the names of the chemical compounds meant nothing. Most American homeowners did not even know what was in the bug sprays they squirted to kill flies and ants in the kitchen or sprayed over rosebushes to kill thrips

and aphids. Nor did it occur to them to think about how strong the poison might be.

Spraying houseflies and lawns was one thing. The bigger danger was in the widespread spraying of fields of wheat and corn that would be made into food for people and animals. The chemical industry was large and growing, and it was "sinister," Rachel Carson wrote in *Silent Spring*. The chemicals were poisoning the environment and causing diseases such as cancer in people. Traces of the poisons remained in corn, in the beef cattle that ate the corn, and in the people who ate the beef. The chemicals seeped into the ground and eventually into rivers and public water supplies. Contamination showed up in the milk of dairy cows who fed on sprayed feed and pastures.

*Time* magazine published a review of *Silent Spring*. The reviewer called the book "a real shocker." But, he added, much of what Rachel Carson had written was an exaggeration and distortion of the facts. He accused Carson of intentionally trying to scare the American public using emotionally charged words and examples. He called her statements that chemicals poisoned human life "nonsense." Some angry readers of her book called her a Communist. So what if birds and fish died? wrote one reader to *Time* magazine. People could live without birds, but they couldn't live without jobs, and the chemical industry was good for the U.S. economy. One government critic called her a "spinster," an insulting term for an unmarried woman. Although Carson was a scientist, the critic questioned her right to write about genetics and birth defects if she herself had never had children. Others declared she was a hysterical female who was a "fanatic about nature." Despite that she listed fifty-five pages of sources in her book, a physician wrote in a medical journal that her scientific conclusions were "so much hogwash."

*Silent Spring* infuriated the chemical industry. And it fought back—hard. "Silent Spring Is Now Noisy Summer: Pesticide Industry Up in Arms Over a New Book," reported the *New York Times*. The chemical industry threatened to sue the magazine that first published Carson's findings. The publisher responded, "Everything in those articles has been checked and is true. Go ahead and sue."

The Monsanto chemical company fought back in another way—publishing a booklet it titled *The Desolate Year*. In this publication, the company predicted a very different kind of spring should the country suddenly stop using chemicals. Harvests would fail. People would starve. Diseases carried by mosquitoes and rats would infect and kill populations. By protesting so loudly, however, the chemical companies drew even more attention to Carson's frightening predictions.

The majority of the people who read *Silent Spring* were shocked but supportive of Carson's ideas. They had not known, they said, how toxic the chemicals were or of the link between pesticides and a poisoned environment.

Writing the book was the most important thing she had ever done in her life, Carson insisted. She knew a single book could not save the planet, but she said, "If I didn't at least try I could never be happy again in nature. But now I can believe that I have at least helped a little."

Her book did more than just "a little." Despite critics' efforts to belittle Carson's

"Everything in those articles has been checked and is true. Go ahead and sue."

—Houghton Mifflin publishing company, referring to *Silent Spring*, 1962

reputation as a scientist, President Kennedy ordered an investigation into environmental pollution. Eventually, Congress banned the

# Sputnik in Space

The space race had begun on October 4, 1957, when the Soviet Union launched a beach-ball-sized satellite into orbit around Earth. The Soviets called the satellite *Sputnik I*. In Russian *sputnik* means "fellow traveler." Four weeks later, the Communist country launched a much larger second *Sputnik* into orbit. This craft carried a living creature, a dog named Laika. The Soviets knew the dog would not survive the journey. The successful orbits shocked the world but especially worried Americans. If the Communists could launch a satellite into orbit, then surely they could fire missiles across an ocean to attack the United States. The Cold War got colder. Americans dug in with new determination to launch a satellite of their own and something more—a spacecraft to carry a human in an orbital flight around Earth.

The government formed the National Aeronautics and Space Administration (NASA) to oversee its piloted spaceflight program. NASA invited applicants to apply to be astronauts. The requirements stated that all applicants be less than 5 feet 11 inches (180 cm) and between twenty-four and forty years of age. They had to have a college degree and experience in mathematics, engineering, or piloting airplanes. And they had to be male. The applicants underwent a series of physically and psychologically grueling tests to measure their ability to endure severe environmental conditions and to think clearly under stress or in emergencies. After two years of testing and narrowing the pool of applicants, NASA proudly presented its Mercury 7 astronauts to the public.

powerful chemical DDT, due in part to Carson's warnings in *Silent Spring*. In 1970 the government created the Environmental Protection Agency (EPA). One of its responsibilities was to investigate and control the use of chemicals. Carson would have welcomed such a government agency had she lived. She died of cancer in 1964, two years after her book was published.

## The Women of Mercury 13

The Cold War continued, but the battlefield became space. And the Mercury 7 astronauts, selected after grueling physical and psychological tests, were the United States' first new Cold War warriors. They were media heroes even before President Kennedy announced in 1961 his goal to land a man on the moon by the end of the decade. The publishers of *Time* and *Life* magazines signed a contract with the newly formed National Aeronautics Space Administration to report on the astronauts and their personal lives. Photographs of the men and their families appeared on the cover of the magazines. In these news stories, reporters compared the seven to the great explorers of the past—Columbus, Magellan, and Daniel Boone. One strategy in winning the war against the Communists was dominating the skies. Mercury 7 was the United States' hope to win the race for space and, in doing so, win the Cold War.

Another team of astronaut warriors was also undergoing the same rigorous tests. The scientists administering the tests called this team the Fellow Lady Astronaut Trainees, or FLAT. The very idea of a woman being shot into space was so fantastic that their training began somewhat in secrecy.

Two scientists, Dr. William Randolph (Randy) Lovelace II and Brigadier General Donald Flickinger, believed that women might be better candidates than men for space travel. Despite popular beliefs that women were frail, these scientists believed women tolerated pain, heat, cold, and even loneliness better or at least as well as men. The real advantage to a woman astronaut, however, was her size. Women are generally lighter than men and so require less oxygen and water. That difference could mean an easier launch into space.

> Despite popular beliefs that women were frail, Dr. Lovelace and Brigadier General Flickinger believed women tolerated pain, heat, cold, and even loneliness better or at least as well as men.

To test their theories, Lovelace and Flickinger recruited a dynamic young female pilot. Between 1957 and 1960, Jerrie Cobb had set four world aviation records for speed, distance, and altitude. She was just twenty-eight years old, but she had been flying since she was twelve and had thousands of flying hours in her logbook. Lovelace invited her to come to his clinic in New

Mexico to undergo tests for possible astronaut training. She enthusiastically agreed. Cobb's participation as a test subject, however, was top secret.

The first tests were medical: X-rays, electrocardiograms, blood work, and urine analysis. Cobb was in excellent health. Next came more complicated procedures. A doctor injected cold water into Cobb's inner ear to test her endurance of dizziness. Cobb pedaled on a bicycle until exhausted, breathing into a mouthpiece that recorded the amount of oxygen she inhaled and the amount of carbon dioxide she exhaled. She lay on her back in a tubelike capsule. It was so narrow that she could not turn or bend her knees. She did not succumb to claustrophobia. Strapped into a gyroscope machine, Cobb was twisted, rolled, and pitched up and down. The Mercury 7 astronauts had nicknamed this machine the vomit comet. Cobb's task was to maintain the controls despite the spinning and somersaulting movements. The test ride lasted forty-five minutes. With each test she passed, Cobb became more determined to become an astronaut.

Next up were the intelligence and psychological tests. No human had ever traveled in outer space, and scientists could only speculate at the hazards of that severe environment. To re-create the dark silence and weightlessness of space, the scientists created

*Jerrie Cobb is shown in 1960 undergoing one of the rigorous tests that male Mercury 7 astronauts were required to take. These included X-rays and a four-hour eye exam. The doctors had the astronauts swallow a rubber tube so that doctors could test their stomach acids. Using an electrical pulse, the physicians tested nerve reflexes in their arms. Ice water was shot into their ears to create vertigo (dizziness) so that the doctors could time how quickly they recovered.*

an isolation tank test. Each of the Mercury 7 astronauts had endured this test too. Then it was Cobb's turn. The scientists placed her in a tank of water with inflated rubber tubes under her neck and around her waist, and they left her there. They watched, and they listened. Hours passed. Would she hallucinate as some of the male test applicants had? She did not. She had no way of knowing how much time had passed. When she finally asked to come out of the tank, they told her she had been inside for almost ten hours.

Jerrie Cobb's performance in the same tests that the Mercury 7 had passed proved that she was qualified both physically and psychologically for the astronaut program. But Cobb was just one woman. If the tests were to be valid, other women had to perform equally well. Lovelace recruited additional test applicants. Thirteen women (the Mercury 13) eventually qualified. Among them was Jane Hart, the wife of Senator Philip Hart of Michigan. She was forty-one years old and the mother of eight children. The youngest FLAT to qualify was twenty-three-year-old Wally Funk, an army flight instructor at Fort Sill, Oklahoma. At the time, few people in the United States knew about the FLAT. "We were the best kept secret in the United States," Funk said.

American's fascination with the Mercury 7 continued, due in part to the publicity contract between NASA and the publishers of *Time* and *Life*. NASA did not welcome publicity about its women trainees, however. In general, society believed that men flew aircraft and spacecraft while women stayed at home. When the media began printing stories about woman astronauts, the backlash was harsh and quick. Just days before the women were to report to Florida for astronaut training, NASA abruptly ended the program. Stunned, the FLAT fought back. Jane Hart appealed to Vice President Lyndon

*Jane Hart* (right), *who held many aviation records and was married to a powerful senator, met with Vice President Lyndon Johnson to make the case for opening astronaut training to women. Johnson listened to Hart and Jerrie Cobb* (left), *who had accompanied Hart to the meeting. He then slipped a note to his assistant to say that the interview should be stopped now!*

*Jackie Cochran, shown here in 1956 at the controls of her private plane, set more speed and altitude records than any other pilot of her era—male or female. Flying did not start out as her main interest. She originally got her pilot's license so that she could sell her line of cosmetics across the country.*

Johnson for an explanation. The Soviet Union was training women, the FLAT argued. So should the Americans.

In 1962 Jerrie Cobb and Jane Hart succeeded in having their case presented before a congressional committee. Earlier that year, John Glenn had completed three orbits in the spacecraft *Friendship 7*. But that was just the beginning of the U.S. space program, Hart told the committee. If women were qualified, they should be part of the program. The women had passed the same tests as the men, and some had performed better than the Mercury 7. If the United States truly wanted to win the space race, then it had to use the most qualified individuals—male or female.

Award-winning pilot Jackie Cochran, who had been the first woman to break the sound barrier in the 1950s, made her statement before the committee. She had enthusiastically supported the women's training. She herself dreamed of flying in space. But, she admitted, setting up a special program just for women astronauts was costly. To spend all that time and money training a woman who might eventually marry, have children, and drop out of the program could jeopardize the entire Mercury program. Cobb and the other FLAT could not believe what they heard. Cochran had been a pioneering aviatrix. The FLAT felt as if she had betrayed them.

In the end, it might have been only a technicality that grounded the Mercury 13 and put an end to their dreams of spaceflight.

# The Soviet Seagull

TASS, the official news agency of the Soviet Union, reported in June 1963 that a "brilliant star" had appeared in the skies above Earth. "It outshines all the film stars in the world. Never and in no country did women ever attain such height."

The brilliant star was the Soviet cosmonaut Valentina Vladimirovna Tereshkova, the first woman to travel in space. Her radio call sign was CHAYKA, which means "seagull." Her adventure lasted three days. The Soviet Union had once again surged forward in the race for space. A white dove was embroidered on Tereshkova's space suit, TASS reported. She had "cornflower blue eyes," and when her spaceship splashed down to Earth, she had bruised her nose. Otherwise, the cosmonaut was in perfect physical condition.

*The world's first female astronaut, Valentina Tereshkova* (above), *was chosen by Soviet premier Nikita Khrushchev because he liked the way she looked and because he wanted someone with a working-class background. The flight did not go well. It would be another nineteen years before the Soviet Union had another female astronaut.*

In the United States, the idea of a woman in space seemed far-fetched and foolish. The *Dallas Morning News* headline on June 17 stated "Russian Blonde Spins around Earth." In defining the cosmonaut as "a blonde," the newspaper editors signaled their attitude toward women. None of the articles on the Mercury 7 astronauts had ever defined them by the color of their hair.

Tereshkova's flight both elated and frustrated the rejected Fellow Lady Astronaut Trainees. Any one of them could have become the first woman in space if only NASA and the congressional committee members had given their thumbs-up. Author and politician Clare Boothe Luce wrote in *Life* magazine, "We must stop trying to make paper dolls of our women." Women were not frail like paper. They were not cutout images to dress up and show off. The United States' refusal to recognize and tap the talents of women was, in her opinion, a "Cold War blunder."

"They never gave us a chance to prove ourselves," said Wally Funk. Still, she hoped that the brilliant Soviet star might change minds at NASA and that the training for the FLAT would begin again.

NASA had required all astronauts to be graduates of military jet test piloting programs and to have college degrees in engineering. Women could not meet these qualifications because the military barred women from becoming test pilots of jet planes. Until women could win equal opportunities to serve in the military, they could never become astronauts.

A few months later, in October 1962, President Kennedy presented the Collier Trophy to the Mercury 7. The trophy was awarded to an individual or a group of people who had made a significant advancement in aviation. During the award ceremony in the White House Rose Garden, President Kennedy said he hoped the award would stimulate others to carry the U.S. flag to the moon and beyond. The Soviet Union might have beaten the United States in launching the first satellite, the first man, and even the first woman to orbit Earth. But there was still the moon to shoot for. Project Mercury had completed its mission. Next up was the Gemini mission and a new team of astronauts. After them would come the Apollo mission. Throughout the 1960s, the FLAT watched and waited for their turn.

## One Small Step for Man...

The 1960s space missions—Mercury, Gemini, and Apollo—had at last fulfilled an idealistic president's goal. On July 20, 1969, the first human stepped on the moon. He was astronaut Neil Armstrong. He had planned what he would say, knowing a satellite would transmit his image and voice from the moon back to Earth. It would reach into the living rooms of families not just in the United States but around the globe. Armstrong said, "One small step for man, one giant leap for mankind." The U.S. astronauts planted a plaque on the moon's surface that read: "Here men from the planet Earth first set foot upon the Moon, June 1969 A.D. We came in peace for all mankind." The United States had beaten the Soviet Union in the space race.

"It should have been me," said Jerrie Cobb.

At least, that is what some people believe Cobb said on the summer evening when she learned that Apollo astronauts Neil Armstrong and Buzz Aldrin had landed on the moon. Approximately 600 million people around the globe witnessed on their television sets the moment when Armstrong leaped off the lunar module's ladder into the powdery dust of the moon's surface.

Jerrie Cobb did not. The former astronaut trainee was in the Amazon jungle of South America, where there were no televisions. She was flying food, medicine, and other supplies to remote outposts, though none quite as remote as the moon. Cobb still felt the disappointment of being dismissed from the astronaut training program because she was a woman. Even so, that evening in the jungle, she danced for joy at the news that Americans had reached the moon.

> Jerrie Cobb felt the disappointment of being dismissed from the astronaut training program because she was a woman. Even so, that evening in the jungle, she danced for joy at the news that Americans had reached the moon.

Although Cobb and the other FLAT were not present in NASA's Mission Control Center in Houston, Texas, they had been—for a short time—a part of the team. That night in the jungle, the moon was closer to Earth than it had ever been. Cobb hoped that one day she might yet climb into a space capsule and take the ride of her life. Not until 1983, however, would the first U.S. female astronaut travel in space. She was Sally Ride, not Jerrie Cobb.

## A Nation at War with Itself— the Vietnam Dilemma

The Cold War had lasted for two decades. In this war, the United States' enemy was the Communists—whether in the Soviet Union, in Korea, or in Vietnam. Since 1964 U.S. soldiers had been fighting in Vietnam.

# The Invisible Women of Vietnam

Cathy Leroy was a freelance photographer. As a freelancer, she didn't work for any one publication. In 1968 she paid her own way to Saigon, South Vietnam. She snapped photographs and sold them to news agencies for fifteen dollars a piece. She was just 5 feet tall (152 cm), weighed 85 pounds (39 kg), and wore her long blonde hair in pigtails. She'd do just about anything to get a good news photograph, including making a combat jump with the 173rd Airborne into the jungle. The morning after her jump, Brigadier General John R. Dean pinned paratroop wings with a gold star on her fatigues. The gold star signified that she had made a combat jump. "Soldiers about to protest having a woman along in combat do a double take when they spot a gold star," reported *Life* magazine.

In 1968 Jane A. Lombardi earned the Bronze Star for her courageous work evacuating a combat hospital in Da Nang, South Vietnam. She was the first woman ever to receive

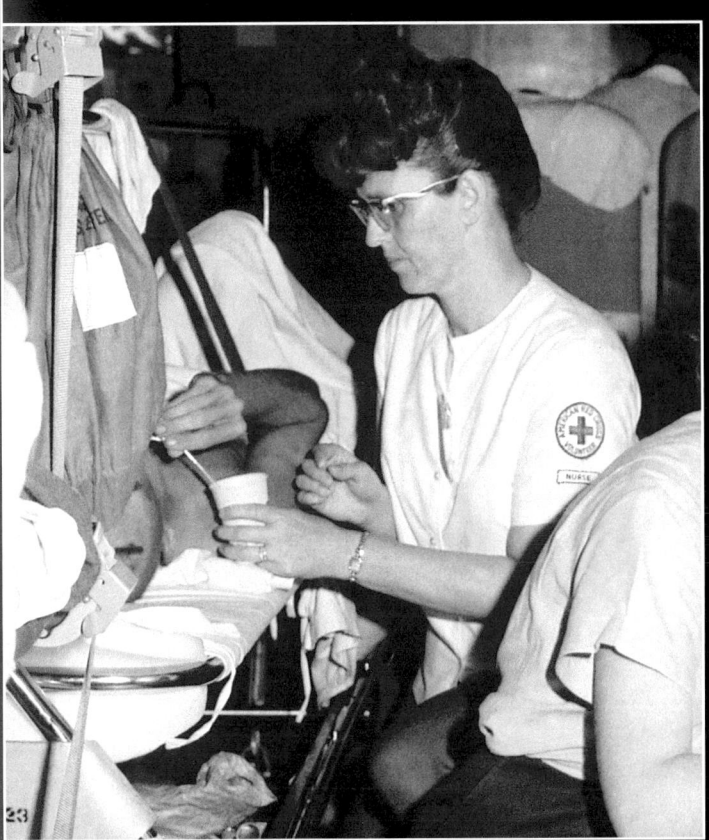

a combat citation. Nurse First Lieutenant Hedwig (Heddy) Orlowski died in 1967 when her plane crashed into a mountainside near Pleiku, Vietnam. She was twenty-three years old. Orlowski's best friend, Penny Kettlewell, also serving as a nurse in Vietnam, planned a memorial service for her. The chief nurse canceled the service. "She said we had no business grieving when we were supposed to be working," said Kettlewell. Women weren't supposed to die in Vietnam. The contributions of these women—the war correspondents, the combat nurses, and the Red Cross volunteers—did not make headlines.

*A nurse attends to a wounded American soldier at South Vietnam's Tan Son Nhut Air Base, January 11, 1967.*

And many died in this small country in Southeast Asia. Night after night, television cameras brought graphic scenes of war into the living rooms of American families. Vietnam was the first televised war. Each night on the evening news, Americans watched soldiers on patrol wadding through rice paddies. They saw the rocket attacks and fire bombs that incinerated jungle foliage and villages. They heard the rapid fire of machine guns and the thudding rotors of rescue helicopters.

What Americans did not see on the nightly news were the women who served in Vietnam—the thousands of nurses in camouflage fatigues, combat boots, and helmets. The soldiers were male. In the 1960s, the U.S. military prohibited enlisted women from combat missions. Women served not only as nurses but also as secretaries, typists, journalists, and intelligence officers. Their stories, however, did not make the evening news.

As the war continued, year after year, the number of American dead and wounded soared. The war divided the nation. Those who supported it believed that if Vietnam fell to Communist forces, then soon after other countries in Asia would also fall, like dominoes one after the other. They believed the spread of Communism anywhere in the world was a threat to democracy at home. Those against the war argued that Vietnam was in the midst of a civil war and that the United States should not interfere in that country's struggle. They rejected the "domino theory" of Communist aggression.

"Hell no, we won't go! Hell no, we won't go!"

—antiwar college student chant, 1968

By 1968 the debate over what to do in Vietnam grew violent. Antiwar protesters staged peace marches and demonstrations in U.S. cities and on college campuses. Both sides—those for and those against the war—clashed in the streets. Television cameras brought this fighting too into living rooms. Americans watched male college students burning their military draft cards. They heard them chanting, "Hell no, we won't go!"

*Carrying graphic anti-Vietnam War posters, members of Women Strike for Peace push their way to the doors of the Pentagon building in February 1967. The main doors of the building (headquarters of the Department of Defense in Washington, D.C.) were locked for thirty minutes as the women attempted to storm it.*

They saw police in riot gear firing tear gas into crowds who refused to clear public areas. In 1969 the United States was a country at war. The enemy was no longer the Communists.

Women, too, were part of these war protests, just as they had taken active roles in civil rights demonstrations and in peace marches to end nuclear testing. Women were there, though the media did not often focus its lens on them directly. More often than not, the lens focused on the men who stood at the microphone or who shouted to the crowd from the steps of buildings. When women tried to take their turn at the microphone, reported antiwar protester Ellen Willis, the men hissed, laughed, and mocked them, drowning out their voices.

And so it often is in popular culture. The stories and images the media portrays are windows to understanding the past. However, so often what is not shown is as revealing as what is. The women warriors of the Cold War did not often make front-page news. They were not the subject of television dramas or movies. Their glossy images did not appear on the cover of popular magazines. That would change, however. By the time the last U.S. soldier returned home from Vietnam—in 1975—the Gidgets and warrior women would launch a new war. This time the protest was for equal rights . . . for women.

# *a* epilogue
# year of protests, 1968

*Sexism is no less evil than racism or capitalism.*

—Ellen Willis, Letter to the Editor, *New York Times*, 1969

*Anti-Vietnam War demonstrators in Washington, D.C., march from the Lincoln Memorial to the Pentagon on October 21, 1967.*

*the year 1968 began with the hope for peace—*

peace in Vietnam and in U.S. cities. The war in Southeast Asia had divided the country. Thousands of U.S. servicemen had died in combat. Images of the war and its victims—both American and Vietnamese—appeared on the nightly television news and in newsmagazines such as *Life* and *Time*. Protesters at home marched in the streets and on college campuses, demanding an end to the war.

Racial tension had also divided the country. Four years earlier, President Lyndon Johnson had signed into law the Civil Rights Act of 1964. Discrimination based on race, color, religion, sex, and national origin was against the law. But the law did not end prejudice. Laws may control behavior, but they cannot erase beliefs and feelings. In some communities, angry mobs still harassed and beat African Americans who attempted to register to vote. Words become law in the few seconds it takes for the president of the United States to sign a bill. But change takes much longer.

The year 1968 was not a year of peace, after all. Wherever people gathered to protest, either against the war in Vietnam or racial injustice, police in riot gear—helmets and shields—patrolled the streets. Television crews with cameras rolling were on the scene too. And then the killing began. On the evening of April 4, an assassin shot civil rights leader Dr. Martin Luther King Jr. The news of his death shattered the African American neighborhoods of many cities across the country. Rioters exploded into the streets, setting fire to buildings and vehicles and looting shops. Two months later, on June 8, an assassin killed Robert Kennedy. The younger brother of John Kennedy, Robert was a candidate for president. He opposed the war in Vietnam. Many who supported his candidacy believed he would end that war if he were elected. But his life had ended just as violently as his brother's had ended five years earlier.

In September 1968, Robin Morgan staged a different kind of protest. It was not against the war in Vietnam. It was not about integrating schools in U.S. cities. The protest focused on sexism, or discrimination against women. Morgan, a published poet as well as an effective activist on behalf of civil rights, lesbian rights, and anti-Vietnam War causes, was a founding member of a woman's rights group called the New York Radical Women (NYRW). The group planned its protest to take place in Atlantic City, New Jersey, on the same day and in the same city where the Miss America Pageant would select its new "ideal woman" from among fifty state contestants. The television cameras and news reporters would already be there to cover the popular beauty pageant. Morgan and hundreds of her fellow radical women would stage quite a different show on the

*Women of the National Women's Liberation Party hold protest signs in front of Convention Hall, where the Miss America Pageant is about to be held in Atlantic City, New Jersey, on September 7, 1968. The picketers are protesting the annual pageant as degrading to women.*

boardwalk. NYRW announced its plans beforehand in a document called "No More Miss America."

The Miss America Pageant was degrading to women, the announcement stated. A beauty pageant was no different from a 4-H Club country fair "where nervous animals are judged for teeth [and] fleece." The pageant was racist too, the document continued. Contestants were limited to white women. "There has never been a Puerto Rican, Alaskan, Hawaiian, or Mexican American winner. Nor has there ever been a true Miss America—an American Indian."

The NYRW welcomed interviews from the press, it stated, but would speak only to women correspondents. Should the Atlantic City police decide to arrest the protesters, they wished to be arrested by female officers. Four hundred women showed up. They tossed what they called woman-garbage into a "freedom can." The garbage included bras; girdles; women's magazines, such as the *Ladies' Home Journal*; mascara; lipsticks; false eyelashes; and curlers. The women carried

*Although not a single bra went up in flames that day, the protest—and the television news coverage of it—sparked a new feminist movement.*

protest signs that read, "Welcome to the cattle auction" and "Miss America is alive and well—in Harlem." Harlem is a predominantly African American section of New York City. The women topped off their protest by crowning a sheep their ideal Miss America.

The women made headlines, but the reporters got the story wrong. Somehow the rumor began that the women had burned their bras in the freedom can. They never did. The radical women from New York might have wanted to, but they had not gotten a fire permit from the city. Still, once the rumor took root, it grew and spread. Popular culture promoted the image of feminists as "bra burning" man haters. Although not a single bra went up in flames that day, the protest—and the television news coverage of it—sparked a new feminist movement. And a new debate. Feminist Ellen Willis would later write in the *New York Times* that she disagreed with Robin Morgan. Yes, sexism was a real problem in the United States, but the oppressors were not those people who operated beauty pageants. It was not the women who wore bathing suits in those pageants, either. It was men, Willis said. "Like any other power group, men will not give up their privileges until they have to."

*the United States in 1968* was a much different country than it had been in the years immediately following the end of World War II. Popular media still created labels and images that told men and women how to dress, behave, and think. But the images had changed, as had the music and fashions. For two decades, the country had survived the threat of the Cold War. Although that threat still existed, much had changed in the United States during those two decades. In 1954 the Senate voted to condemn Senator Joseph McCarthy and his unsubstantiated accusations against others. Senator Margaret Chase Smith ran for the presidential nomination in 1963. She lost, but her campaign offered hope that in the future more women would run for political office.

In the decades to come, women would continue to challenge society's stereotypes. In 1972 Shirley Chisholm, the first African American woman elected to Congress, would make her bid for the presidency. The women of the 1970s, 1980s, and 1990s would gather their courage to continue the fight for racial, sexual, and social justice.

# Source Notes

6 Margaret Chase Smith, quoted in Patricia Ward Wallace, *Politics of Conscience* (Westport, CT: Praeger Publishers, 1995), 104.

7 "Declaration of Conscience," *Margaret Chase Smith Library*, n.d., http://www.mcslibrary.org/program/library/declaration.htm(June 21, 2007).

9 Ibid.

10 Wallace, 107.

10 "As Maine Goes . . ." *Time*, September 5, 1960, n.d. http://www.time.com/time/printout/0,8816,826543,00.html (June 21, 2007)

11 Janann Sherman, *No Place for a Woman: A Life of Senator Margaret Chase Smith* (Piscataway, NJ: Rutgers University Press, 2000), 112.

13 Elaine Tyler May, *Homeward Bound: American Families in the Cold War Era* (New York: Basic Books, 1998), 86.

13 Betty Friedan, *The Feminine Mystique* (New York: W. W. Norton, 1997), 61.

13 May, 86.

14 Ibid., 119.

17 Lynn Peril, *Pink Think: Becoming a Woman in Many Uneasy Lessons* (New York: W. W. Norton, 2002), 3.

18 Ibid., 22–23.

20 *Time*, "Jackie," January 20, 1961, n.d., http://www.time.com/time/magazine/article/0,9171,871957,00.html7x cbf (March 1, 2007).

20 Carl Sferrazza Anthony, *As We Remember Her: Jacqueline Kennedy Onassis in the Words of Her Friends and Family* (New York: Harper Collins, 1997), 41.

20 Jan Pottker, *Janet & Jackie* (New York: St. Martin's Press, 2001), 121.

23 Marriage announcement 3, *New York Times*, June 12, 1955, S8.

23 *Time*, "For Happier Housewives," October 8, 1951, n.d., http://www.time.com/time/magazine/article/0,9171,859393,00.html (March 1, 2007).

24 *Time*, "Just Well Rounded," October 10, 1949, n.d, http://www.time.com/time/magazine/article/0,9171,800939,00.html (March 1, 2007).

26 Friedan, 153.

27 Ibid., 181.

27–28 Judy Yung, *Unbound Feet: A Social History of Chinese Women in San Francisco* (Berkeley: University of California Press, 1995), 119.

28 Ibid.

28 Clifford R. Adams, Making Marriage Work, *Ladies Homes Journal*, February 1955, 26.

28 Ibid.

31 Ibid.

31 Ibid.

34 Peril, 112.

35 *Time*, "All's Swell at Mattel," October 26, 1962, n.d., http://www.time.com/time/magazine/article/0,9171,874558,00.html (March 1, 2007).

36 Ibid.

38 Ted Kreiter, "Audrey Hepburn: A Son's Reflections," L'Ange des Enfants, May–June 2004, n.d., http://www.audrey1.com/articles/articles29.html (March 1, 2007).

38 David Ansen, "A Princess in Disguise," *Newsweek*, February 1, 1993.

39 Sean Hepburn Ferrer, *Audrey Hepburn: An Elegant Spirit* (New York: Atria Books, 2003), 138.

22 *Time*, "New Man in the Ladies' Den," December 2, 1946, n.d., http://www.time.com/time/magazine/article/0,9171,887287,00.html (March 1, 2007).

30 Claudia H. Deutsch, "Dreaming of Bras for the Modern Woman," *New York Times*, September 29, 2005, n.d., http://www.nytimes.com/2005/09/28/business/media/28adco.html?ex=1285560000&en=a992d7ab89e1acf6&ei=5090&partner=rssuserland&emc=rss (March 1, 2007).

29 Robert L. Teague, "Everyone Has Wilma Rudolph on the Run," *New York Times*, February 4, 1961, 11.

33 Ibid., 28.

37 Ruth Handler and Jacqueline Shannon, *Dream Doll: The Ruth Handler Story* (Stamford, CT: Longmeadow Press, 1994), 212–213.

41 Michael Callahan, "Peyton Place's Real Victim," vanityfair.com, n.d., http://www.vanityfair.com/fame/features/2006/03/peytonplace200603?printable=true&currentPage=all (June 11, 2007).

42 Dan Sullivan, "The Games Day People Play," *New York Times*, December 17, 1967, 119.

44  David Halberstam, *The Fifties* (New York: Random House, 1993), 496.

44  Ibid., 501.

45  Donna L. Halper, *Invisible Stars: A Social History of Women in American Broadcasting* (Armonk, NY: M. E. Sharpe, 2001), 158.

46  *Time*, "Troubles & Bubbles," April 15, 1957, n.d., http://www.time.com/time/magazine/article/0,9171,862558,00.html (March 1, 2007).

48  Marcia F. Cassidy, *What Women Watched: Daytime Television in the 1950s* (Austin: University of Texas Press, 2005), 211.

49  Ibid.

51  Aniko Bodroghkozy, "Beulah," *Broadcast Communications*, n.d., http://www.museum.tv/archives/etv/B/htmlB/beulah/beulah.htm (November 8, 2006).

51  Jill Watts, *Hattie McDaniel: Black Ambition, White Hollywood* (NY: HarperCollins, 2005), p. 39.

52–53  Coyne S. Sanders, *Desilu: The Story of Lucille Ball and Desi Arnaz* (New York: Harper Collins, 1993), 26, 91.

53  *Time*, "Moore for Housewives," February 2, 1953, n.d., http://www.time.com/time/magazine/article/0,9171,817877,00.html (March 1, 2007).

54  Debra Michals, "Women on the Way: How Women Entrepreneurs Reshaped the American Economic Landscape in the Wake of World War II," *American Heritage Magazine* 52:4, June 2001, http://www.americanheritage.com/articles/magazine/ah/2001/4/2001_4_87.shtml (June 21, 2007).

54  Stephanie Stoughton, "Take Risks, Vernon Tells Students," *The Virginian-Pilot*, October 16, 1995, 5.

54  Ibid.

55  May, 10.

55  Ibid., 146.

55  Halberstam, 724.

58  Friedan, 69.

58  Ibid., 71.

59  Ibid.

59  Ibid., 37.

59  Lucy Freeman, "'The Feminine Mystique,'" *New York Times*, April 7, 1963, n.d., http://www.nytimes.com/1963/04/07/books/friedan-feminine.html (March 1, 2007).

61  Ibid.

61  Friedan, 380.

61  Ibid., 7.

62  Susan Douglas, *Where the Girls Are: Growing Up Female with the Mass Media* (New York: Random House, 1994), 87.

64  *Time*, Letters, July 9, 1956, n.d., http://www.time.com/time/magazine/article/0,9171,893435,00.html (March 1, 2007).

65  *Newsweek*, "The Dreamy Teen-Age Market," September 1957, 94.

67  Deanne Stillman, "The Real Gidget," in *Surf Culture*, n.d., http://www.californiaauthors.com/essay_stillman.shtml (March 1, 2007).

67  Ibid.

68  David Emery, "The Hook: An Urban Legend," *About.com*, n.d., http://urbanlegends.about.com/od/horrors/a/the_hook.htm?iam=dpile_100 (June 21, 2007).

69  Stillman.

70  Ibid.

72  Frank Page and Joey Kent, "Elvis at the Louisiana Hayride," in *Something in the Water*, available online at the *Rockabilly Hall of Fame Website*, n.d., http://www.rockabillyhall.com/ElvisHayride1.html (March 1, 2007).

72  Ibid.

73  Peter B. Levy, ed., *America in the Sixties—Right, Left and Center: A Documentary History* (Westport, CT: Praeger, 1998), 168.

73–75  John Grochowski, "Beatlemaniacs Love Them Do," *Chicago Sun-Times*, September 2, 2004, n.d., http://www.findarticles.com/p/articles/mi_qn4155/is_20040902/ai_n12560773 (November 8, 2006).

73  Ibid.

76  Douglas, 92.

77  Stephen Holden, "With Ellie Greenwich, the Bottom Line Is Fun," *New York Times*, January 20, 1984, n.d. http://movies2.nytimes.com/mem/movies/review.html?res=9801E2D81E38F933A15752C0A962948260 (June 21, 2007).

77  Douglas, 90.

77  Ron Fell, "Carole King: Rewriting Her Legacy," *Gavin Report*, April 21, 1989, n.d., http://www.willybrauch.de/In_Their_Own_Words/caroleking.htm (November 8, 2006).

77  Douglas.

79   Herb Boyd, "Motown's Maven of Style," *Black World Today*, November 8, 2003, January 23, 2004, http://www.tbwt.org/index.php?option=content&task=view&id=20&Itemid=41 (November 8, 2006).

79   Mike Murphy, "Song of Etiquette," *Metrotimes*, March 15–21, 2006, n.d., http://www.metrotimes.com/editorial/story.asp?id=5453 (November 8, 2006).

81   *Time*, "The Cockney Kid," November 11, 1966, n.d., http://www.time.com/time/magazine/article/0,9171,843028,00.html (March 1, 2007).

78   Rachel Leibrock, "'You Don't Own Me' Is Still Gore's Motto," *Sacramento Bee*, April 14, 2006, n.d., http://www.shns.com/shns/g_index2.cfm?action=detail&pk=LESLEYGORE-04-14-06 (November 8, 2006).

84   Rosa Parks, *Quiet Strength* (Grand Rapids, MI: Zonderan Pub., 1994), 17.

86   "Elizabeth Ann Eckford," *Encyclopedia of Arkansas*, November 2, 2006, http://movies2.nytimes.com/mem/movies/review.html?res=9801E2D81E38F933A15752C0A962948260 (June 21, 2007).

86–87   Halberstam, 676.

87   Benjamin Fine, "Arkansas Troops Bar Negro Pupils; Governor Defiant," *New York Times*, September 3, 1957, 1.

87–88   Ibid.

88   *Time*, "Making a Crisis in Arkansas, September 16, 1957, n.d., http://www.time.com/time/magazine/article/0,9171,809859,00.html (March 1, 2007).

90   *Ebony*, March 1999.

91   Elizabeth Brown-Gillory, *Their Place on the Stage: Black Women Playwrights in America*. (Westport, CT: Praeger, 1990) 35.

91   Alice Bernstein, "Philip Rose: A Broadway Journey Against Racism," *Afro-Americans in New York Life and History*, January 2005, n.d., http://findarticles.com/p/articles/mi_m0SAF/is_1_29/ai_n12417353 (November 8, 2006).

92   Benjamin Ivry, "You Can't Do that on Broady! A *Raisin in the Sun* and Other Theatrical Improbabilities," *American Theater*, October 2001, 120.

93   "Fannie Lou Hamer's Testimony before the Credentials Committee of the Democratic National Convention of 1964," *Mississippi Becomes a Democracy*, n.d. http://democracy.soundprint.org/FLHTestimony.php (June 21, 2007).

94   Dan Olson, "The Mondale Lectures: Atlantic City Revisited," *Minnesota Public Radio*, February 28, 2007, http://news.minnesota.publicradio.org/features/2000,02/11_olsond_mondalelectures (March 1, 2007).

94   Ibid.

96   Rosa Parks ,quoted in Gail Collins, *America's Women: 400 Years of Dolls, Drudges, Helpmates, and Heroines* (New York: Harper Collins, 2003), 430.

97   Lottie Joiner, "Down in the Delta," *New Crisis*, March–April 2002, n.d., http://findarticles.com/p/articles/mi_qa3812/is_200203/ai_n9055762 (November 8, 2006).

97   Dick Schapp, "Secret Project in Mississippi—Interracial Meetings of Women," *New York Herald Tribune*, August 30, 1964, n.d., http://www.people.virginia.edu/~hcs8n/WIMS/frame-history.html (November 8, 2006).

97   Riane Eisler, "Toward an Economics of Caring: A Conversation with Dr. Riane Eisler," *Newsletter of the Boston Research Center*, n.d., http://www.partnership-way.org/html/subpages/articles/economics.htm (June 21, 2007)

97   "Wednesdays in Mississippi: 1964–1965 Final Report," 32, *Wednesday's Women*, n.d., http://people.virginia.edu/~hcs8n/WIMS/frame-wedwomen.html (April 30, 2007).

98   Marcia M. Gallo, *Different Daughters: A History of the Daughters of Bilitis and the Rise of Lesbian Activism* (New York: Carroll & Graf, 2006), 86.

99   Vicki Kemper, "A Citizen for All Seasons—Consumer Advocate Esther Peterson," *Common Cause*, Spring 1995, n.d, http://www.findarticles.com/p/articles/mi_m1554/is_n1_v21/ai_16791411 (November 8, 2006).

100   Ibid.

100   Ibid.

103   Delia M. Rios, "In Mrs. Kennedy's Pink Suit, an Indelible Memory of Public Grief," *Newhouse News Service*, n.d., http://www.newhousenews.com/archive/Rios111303.html (November 8, 2006).

104   *Another Mother for Peace*, n.d., http://www.anothermother.org/history.html (March 1, 2007).

105   Gerald G. Gross, "A-Bomb Sinks 2 Ships and Damages 17," *Washington Post*, July 1, 1946, n.d., http://www.washingtonpost.com/wp-srv/inatl/longterm/flash/july/bikini46.htm (November 8, 2006).

105 Matin Zuberi, "Operation Crossroads: Meeting the Bomb at Close Quarters," Strategic Analysis 22:11, February 1999, n.d., http://www.ciaonet.org/olj/sa_99zum01.html (March 1, 2007).

106 Ibid.

107 Mary Learson Sharmat, "Mary Sharmat's Statement Regarding Her Civil Defense Protest," *The American Experience*, n.d., http://www.pbs.org/wgbh/amex/bomb/filmmore/reference/primary/sharmat.html (March 1, 2007).

108 Ibid.

108 Ibid.

108 Ibid.

108 Ibid.

108 Ibid.

108 Ibid.

109 May, *Witness to War*, 109.

109 Speakers' booklet on Marguerite Higgins published by The Executives' Club of Chicago, 1953.

110 Lisa Swerdlow, "Ladies' Day at the Capitol: Women Strike for Peace *versus* HUAC," in *Unequal Sisters: A Multicultural Reader in U.S. Women's History, edited by Ellen Carol Dubois and Vicki L. Ruiz* (New York: Routledge, 1990), 400.

110 Ibid.

110 *Newsweek*, November 13, 1961, 21, as quoted in Swerdlow, 401.

113 Ibid., 413.

114 Rachel Carson, *Silent Spring* (New York: Houghton Mifflin, 1994), 3.

115 *Time*, "Pesticides: The Price for Progress," September 28, 1962, n.d., http://www.time.com/time/magazine/article/0,9171,940091,00.html (March 1, 2007).

151 Michael Jay Friedman, "Rachel Carson: A Book that Changed a Nation," March 2007, http://usinfo.state.gov/products/pubs/carson/friedman.htm (June 21, 2007).

116 Frank Graham Jr., *Since Silent Spring* (Boston: Random House, 1993), 50, 56.

116 Laura Orlando, "Industry Attacks on Dissent: From Rachel Carson to Oprah," *Dollars and Sense*, April 19, 2002, n.d., http://www.dollarsandsense.org/archives/2002/0302orlando.html (November 8, 2006).

116 Peter Matthiessen, "Environmentalist," *Time*, March 29, 1999, http://www.time.com/time/magazine/article/0,9171,990622,00.html (June 21, 2007).

116 Orlando.

120 Sam Burbank, "Mercury 13's Wally Funk Fights for Her Place in Space," *National Geographic Today*, July 9, 2003, n.d., http://news.nationalgeographic.com/news/2003/07/0709_030709_tvspacewoman.html (November 8, 2006).

109 Antoinette May, *Witness to War: A Biography of Marguerite Higgins, the Legendary Pulitzer Prize-Winning War Correspondent* (New York: Penguin, 1983), 154.

122 *Time*, "Women Are Different," June 28, 1963, n.d., http://www.time.com/time/magazine/article/0,9171,874956,00.html (March 1, 2007).

122 Nolen, 264.

123 "Neil Armstrong," N.A.S.A., n.d., http://www.nasa.gov/worldbook/armstrong_neil_worldbook.html (June 21, 2007).

123 *Apollo Information Flight summary*, n.d. http://www-pao.ksc.nasa.gov/kscpao/history/apollo/flight-summary.htm (June 21, 2007).

123 Nolen, x.

125 George P. Hunt, "A Tiny Girl with Paratroopers' Wings," *Life*, February 16, 1968, 3.

125 Laura Palmer, "The Nurses of Vietnam, Still Wounded," *New York Times Magazine*, November 7, 1993, 41.

128 Ellen Willis, "Women, Revolution, Sexism, Etc., Etc.," *New York Times*, March 2, 1969, SM6.

130 *Chicago Women's Liberation Union Herstory Project*, "What was the Chicago Women's Liberation Union?" n.d., http://www.cwluherstory/index.html (November 8, 2006).

131 Willis, SM6.

# Selected Bibliography

Adams, Clifford R. "Making Marriage Work," *Ladies' Home Journal*, January 1950 and February 1955, 26+.

Anthony, Carl Sferrazza. *As We Remember Her: Jacqueline Kennedy Onassis in the Words of Her Friends and Family*. New York: Harper Collins, 1997.

Bailey, Beth L. *From Front Porch to Back Seat: Courtship in Twentieth-Century America*. Baltimore: Johns Hopkins University Press, 1989.

Banet-Weiser, Sarah. *The Most Beautiful Girl in the World*. Berkeley: University of California Press, 1999.

Basinger, Jeanine. *A Woman's View: How Hollywood Spoke to Women 1930–1960*. New York: Knopf, 1993.

Bradford, Sarah. *America's Queen: The Life of Jacqueline Kennedy Onassis*. New York: Viking, 2000.

Brumberg, Joan Jacobs. *The Body Project: An Intimate History of American Girls*. New York: Random House, 1997.

Carson, Rachel. *Silent Spring*. New York: Houghton Mifflin Co., 1994.

Cassidy, Marsha F. *What Women Watched: Daytime Television in the 1950s*. Austin: University of Texas Press, 2005.

Collins, Gail. *America's Women: 400 Years of Dolls, Drudges, Helpmates, and Heroines*. New York: Harper Collins, 2003

CONELRAD. "Atomic Honeymooners: Well-Sheltered Love May Last a Lifetime." *CONELRAD*. N.d. http://www.conelrad.com/atomic_honeymooners.html, (November 8, 2006).

Coontz, Stephanie. *The Way We Never Were*. New York: Basic Books, 1992.

Cox, Billy. "Gidget Joins the Peace Corps." *Florida Today*, March 25, 2004. Available online at *Peace Corps Online*. March 29, 2004. http://peacecorpsonline.org/messages/messages/2629/2020450.html (November 8, 2006).

Douglas, Susan. *Where the Girls Are: Growing Up Female with the Mass Media*. New York: Random House, 1994.

Douglas, Susan, and Meredith W. Michaels. *The Mommy Myth: The Idealization of Motherhood and How It Has Undermined All Women*. New York: Free Press, 2004.

Ehrenreich, Barbara, and Deirdre English. *For Her Own Good: Two Centuries of the Experts' Advice to Women*. New York: Anchor Books, 2005.

Friedan, Betty. *The Feminine Mystique*. New York: W. W. Norton, 1997.

Graf, Laura Kunstler. "Sirens, Dog Tags, & P.S. 11: A Cold War Remembrance." *CONELRAD*. July 21, 2003. http://www.conelrad.com/testimony/lauragraff.html (November 8, 2006).

Halberstam, David. *The Fifties*. New York: Random House, 1993.

Halper, Donna L. *Invisible Stars: A Social History of Women in American Broadcasting*. Armonk, NY: M. E. Sharpe, 2001.

Hamamoto, Darrell. *Nervous Laughter: Television Situation Comedy and Liberal Democratic Ideology*. New York: Praeger, 1989.

Hamer, Fannie Lou. "Testimony Before the Credentials Committee, Democratic National Convention," August 22, 1964. *Calvin College, Voice of Freedom*. N.d. http://www.calvin.edu/academic/cas/programs/pauleyg/voices/fhamer.htm (November 8, 2006).

Hendershot, Cyndy. "Monster at the Soda Shop: Teenagers and Fifties Horror Films." *Images: A Journal of Film and Popular Culture*, 2001. http://www.imagesjournal.com/search.htm (November 8, 2006).

Holden, Stephen. "With Ellie Greenwich, the Bottom Line Is Fun." *New York Times*, January 20, 1984. 2007. http://query.nytimes.com/gst/fullpage.html?res=9801E2D81E38F933A15752C0A962948260 (November 8, 2006).

Israel, Betsy. *Bachelor Girl: 100 Years of Breaking the Rules—A Social History of Living Single*. New York: Perennial, 2002.

Kurlansky, Mark. *1968: The Year That Rocked the World*. New York: Random House, 2004.

Landay, Lori. *Madcaps, Screwballs, Con Women: The Female Trickster in American Culture*. Philadelphia: University of Pennsylvania Press, 1998.

Layman, Richard, ed. *American Decades 1950–1959*. Washington, DC: Gale Research, 1994.

Leaming, Barbara. *Mrs. Kennedy: The Missing History of the Kennedy Years*. New York: Touchstone, 2001.

Levy, Peter B., ed. *America in the Sixties—Right, Left and Center: A Documentary History*. Westport, CT: Praeger, 1998.

May, Antoinette. *Witness to War: A Biography of Marguerite Higgins, the Legendary Pulitzer Prize-Winning War Correspondent*. New York: Penguin, 1983.

May, Elaine Tyler. *Homeward Bound: American Families in the Cold War Era*. New York: Basic Books, 1998.

Methvin, Eugene H. *The Riot Makers: The Technology of Social Demolition*. New Rochelle, NY: Arlington House, 1970.

Murphy, Mike. "Song of Etiquette: Maxine Powell Buffed Motown's Rough Edges." *Metrotimes*, March 15–21, 2006. http://www.metrotimes.com (March 1, 2007).

Nolan, Stephanie. *Promised the Moon: The Untold Story of the First Women in the Space Race*. New York: Four Walls Eight Windows, 2002.

Peril, Lynn. *Pink Think: Becoming a Woman in Many Uneasy Lessons*. New York: W. W. Norton, 2002.

Pottker, Jan. *Janet & Jackie*. New York: St. Martin's Press, 2001.

Raymond, Diane, ed. *Sexual Politics and Popular Culture*. Bowling Green, OH: Bowling Green State University Popular Press, 1990.

Reeves, Thomas C. *The Life and Times of Joe McCarthy: A Biography*. New York: Stein and Day, 1982.

Riordan, Teresa. *Inventing Beauty*. New York: Broadway Books, 2004.

Rios, Delia M. "In Mrs. Kennedy's Pink Suit, an Indelible Memory of Public Grief." *Newhouse News Service*. 2003. http://www.newhousenews.com/archive/rios111303.html (November 8, 2006).

Sanders, Coyne S. *Desilu: The Story of Lucille Ball and Desi Arnaz*. New York: Harper Collins, 1993.

Scranton, Philip, ed. *Beauty and Business*. New York: Routledge, 2001.

Sharmat, Mary Learson. "Mary Sharmat's Statement Regarding Her Civil Defense Protest." *American Experience*. N.d. http://www.pbs.org/wgbh/amex/bomb/filmmore/reference/primary/sharmat.html (March 1, 2007).

Sherman, Janann. *No Place for a Woman: A Life of Senator Margaret Chase Smith*. Piscataway, NJ: Rutgers University Press, 2000.

Smith, Margaret Chase. *Declaration of Conscience*. New York: Doubleday and Co., 1972.

Solnit, Rebecca. "Three Who Made a Revolution." *Nation*, April 3, 2006. Available online at *Earth, Peace and Justice*. March 16, 2006. http://www.pej.org/html/modules.php?op=modload&name=News&file=article&sid=4365 (November 8, 2006).

Swerdlow, Amy. "Ladies' Day at the Capitol: Women Strike for Peace Versus HUAC." In *Unequal Sisters: A Multicultural Reader in U.S. Women's History*, edited by Ellen Carol Dubois and Vicki L. Ruiz. New York: Routledge, 1990.

Taylor, Ella. *Prime-Time Families Television Culture in Postwar America*. Berkeley: University of California Press, 1989.

Wallace, Patricia Ward. *Politics of Conscience*. Westport, CT: Praeger Publishers, 1995.

Yeager, Chuck, and Leon Janos. *Yeager: An Autobiography*. New York: Bantam Books, 1985.

# Further Reading and Websites

## BOOKS

Briggs, Carole S. *Women in Space*. Minneapolis: Twenty-First Century Books, 1999.

Gottfried, Ted. *The Fight for Peace: A History of Antiwar Movements in America*. Minneapolis: Twenty-First Century Books, 2006.

Gourley, Catherine. *Media Wizards: A Behind-the-Scenes Look at Media Manipulation*. Minneapolis: Twenty-First Century Books, 1999.

Kuhn, Betsy. *The Race for Space*. Minneapolis: Twenty-First Century Books, 2007.

Levy, Debbie. *The Vietnam War*. Minneaoplis: Twenty-First Century Books, 2004.

Lobenthal, Joel. *Radical Rags: Fashions of the Sixties*. New York: Abbeville Press, 1990.

Miller, Brandon Marie. *Dressed for the Occasion*. Minneapolis: Twenty-First Century Books, 1999.

Sherman, Josepha. *The Cold War*. Minneapolis: Twenty-First Century Books, 2004.

Streissguth, Tom. *Wilma Rudolph*. Minneapolis: Twenty-First Century Books, 2007.

Sullivan, George. *Journalists at Risk: Reporting America's Wars*. Minneapolis: Twenty-First Century Books, 2006.

Wadsworth, Ginger. *Rachel Carson*. Minneapolis: Twenty-First Century Books, 1992.

Weissman, Jenna. *Common Threads: A Parade of American Clothing*. Boston: Little, Brown and Co., 1992.

Zeinert, Karen. *The Valiant Women of the Vietnam War*. Minneapolis: Twenty-First Century Books, 2000.

## WEBSITES

*Advertisements*

The Advertising Century
http://adage.com/century/index.html
Advertising Age presents images and articles on the industry's most meaningful people, events, trends, issues, and controversies. The site includes advertising slogans and icons.

*Cold War*

CONELRAD
http://www.conelrad.com/index.php
In the 1950s, CONELRAD was a national Emergency Broadcasting System outlet available during the early Cold War. The agency provided tips for surviving an atomic attack. The CONELRAD website provides primary sources on the atomic culture of the past, including music, film, photographs, and illustrations relating to surviving an atomic attack.

*Music and Film*

Filmsite.org
http://www.filmsite.org
This award-winning resource for classic films allows users to search the database by either film title or by decade. The site includes very detailed summaries of film plots and also short articles on film genres and how to view film critically.

The History of Rock 'n' Roll
http://www.history-of-rock.com/indx.html
This website provides a timeline that actually begins in the 1870s and continues to the present. A special focus is on what the webmaster called "The Golden Decade—1955 to 1964." The site includes real audio sounds and short biographies of musicians.

## Society and Social Customs

American Cultural History
http://kclibrary.nhmccd.edu/decades.html
Presented by Kingwood College Library and prepared by reference librarians, this site categorizes cultural and historical topics by decades. Research and links to other sites cover a range of subjects, from radio, television, and film to education, economics, and significant events.

The FiftiesWeb
http://www.fiftiesweb.com
Fashions, slang, popular music, classic television program—this site provides more than one thousand pages of articles, photographs, and trivia. Some information on classic television programs of the 1960s and 1970s is also available here.

They Wore America on Their Sleeves
http://xroads.virginia.edu/~MA04/hess/Fashion/
theyworeamericahome.html
This website, also sponsored by the American Cultures project at the University of Virginia, provides information on the relationship between clothes and society. Primary source documents digitalized online include news articles and catalog pages.

## Vietnam War

The History Place Presents: The Vietnam War
http://www.historyplace.com/unitedstates/vietnam
This website provides a timeline of events plus images, quotes and analysis of the war from 1945 through 1975.

# Index

# Photo Acknowledgments

**The images in this book are used with the permission of:**

© Al Fenn/Time Life Pictures/Getty Images, p. 3; © Bettmann/CORBIS, pp. 4, 18 (left), 32 (left), 71, 80 (both), 104, 113, 120, 125, 127, 128; © 2000 Daily News LP, p. 6; AP Photo, pp. 8, 21 (both), 22, 27 (right), 35, 48, 82, 99, 111, 114, 130; AP Photo/Herbert K. Smith, p. 9; © Hulton Archive/Getty Images, pp. 10, 38, 39 (all), 55, 68, 72, 74, 76 (second from right), 78, 81, 122; © American Stock/Hulton Archive/Getty Images, p. 11; National Archives, p. 12; © Capp Enterprises, Inc. Used by permission, p. 13; Private Collection, pp. 14, 26, 30, 32 (right), 33 (both), 60; Courtesy of the Tretter Collection in GLBT Studies, University of Minnesota, p. 15; "HOW TO MARRY A MILLIONAIRE" © 1953 Twentieth Century Fox. All rights reserved. Image provided by Bettmann/CORBIS, p. 16; © Lambert/ Hulton Archive/Getty Images, p. 18 (right); © Morgan Collection/Hulton Archive/Getty Images, p. 19; Library of Congress, pp. 23, 27 (left), 29, 62, 90, 93, 107; © Yale Joel/Time Life Pictures/Getty Images, p. 24; © Lisa Larsen/Time Life Pictures/Getty Images, p. 25 (left); THE AFFAIRS OF DOBIE GILLIS © Turner Entertainment Co. A Warner Bros. Entertainment Company. All Rights Reserved. Image provided by Everett Collection, p. 25 (right); © P.A. NEWS/ CORBIS KIPA, p. 34; © Allan Grant/Time Life Pictures/Getty Images, pp. 37, 69; Courtesy of Universal Studios Licensing, LLLP. Image provided by Photofest, p. 40; © Brown Brothers, pp. 42, 76 (right); © William Gottlieb/CORBIS, p. 43; © H. Armstrong Roberts/ Retrofile/Getty Images, p. 44; © CBS/Landov, pp. 45, 50 (right); Everett Collection, pp. 46, 50 (top left), 51, 63;

Screen Gems/The Kobal Collection, p. 50 (bottom left); © CBS Photo Archive/Hulton Archive/Getty Images, p. 52; Lillian Vernon Corporation Archives, p. 54; From the collections of the Texas/Dallas History and Archives Division, Dallas Public Library, p. 56; Marion O'Brien Donovan Papers, Archives Center, National Museum of American History, Smithsonian Institution, p. 57; © Bettye Lane, p. 58; © Murray Garrett/Hulton Archive/Getty Images, p. 64; © SuperStock, Inc./ SuperStock, p. 65; © Alfred Eisenstaedt/Time Life Pictures/Getty Images, p. 66; © Henry Groskinsky/Time Life Pictures/Getty Images, p. 67; © Frank Driggs Collection/Hulton Archive/Getty Images, p. 76 (left and second from left); © Getty Images, p. 84; © Francis Miller/Time Life Pictures/Getty Images, p. 86; © Joseph Scherschel/Time Life Pictures/Getty Images, p. 89; © Gordon Parks/Time Life Pictures/Getty Images, p. 91; © AFP/Getty Images, p. 95; Star Collection, reprinted by permission of the DC Public Library, © Washington Post, p. 96; Courtesy of Del Martin and Phyllis Lyon, p. 98; Rowland Scherman, Peace Corps/John F. Kennedy Presidential Library, Boston, p. 101; © Ed Clark/Time Life Pictures/Getty Images, p. 102; © Elliot Erwit/Magnum Photos, p. 103; Reprinted with permission of The Buffalo News, Image from the National Archives, p. 106; © Time Life Pictures/ Getty Images, p. 109; © Ralph Crane/Time Life Pictures/Getty Images, p. 119; © Loomis Dean/Time Life Pictures/Getty Images, p. 121.

Front Cover: © Michael Ochs Archives/CORBIS (left); AP Photo (right).

Catherine Gourley is an award-winning author and editor of books for young adults. A former editor of *Read* magazine, Gourley is the national director for Letters About Literature, a reading-writing promotion program of the Center for the Book in the Library of Congress. In addition, she is the curriculum writer for The Story of Movies, an educational outreach program on film study and visual literacy in the middle school developed by The Film Foundation, Los Angeles.

Among Gourley's more than 20 books are *Media Wizards* and *Society's Sisters* as well as the other four volumes in the Images and Issues of Women in the Twentieth Century series—*Gibson Girls and Suffragists: Perceptions of Women from 1900 to 1918*; *Flappers and the New American Woman: Perceptions of Women from 1918 through the 1920s*; *Rosie and Mrs. America: Perceptions of Women in the 1930s and 1940s*; and *Ms. and the Material Girls: Perceptions of Women from the 1970s through the 1990s*.